How To Survive Owning A Recording Studio

How To Survive Owning A Recording Studio

BZ Lewis

Studio 132 Publishing

2015

First Printing: 2015

ISBN 978-1-312-53455-1

Studio 132 Publishing
6802 Gunn Drive
Oakland, CA 94611

www.studio132.com

Dedication

This book is dedicated to the many teachers I've had over the years. Where would I be without you?

Contents

Acknowledgements

I would like to thank my parents Tumbleweed Smith and Susan Lewis for being so supportive in my musical pursuits, my brother Kevin for showing me a few chords on guitar when I was young, my classical teachers Marshall Horn and Adam Holtzman. The cover picture was taken at Ninth Street Opus studio..

HOW TO SURVIVE OWNING A RECORDING STUDIO

By BZ Lewis

A note from your author

Who is BZ Lewis?

There's a joke in the music business about the four stages of an artist's career. 1: Who is BZ Lewis? 2: Get me BZ Lewis, 3: Get me a young BZ Lewis, and finally, 4: Who is BZ Lewis?

I seem to be a bit of a contradiction. I've had incredible success in the music biz, but only a handful of people have heard of me. I've worked with some of the biggest names in the business and on platinum selling titles, yet my more notable clients are corporate and video game companies despite the majority of my time being spent with local artists and bands. My compositions have been broadcast all over the world, but few people would even know that they heard it, much less actually know the name of the guy who is behind the music.

Just so you know about whom you're reading, here are some highlights from my credit list: I'm a six-time Emmy Award winning composer/producer. I've licensed music for World Poker Tour, Burn Notice, NBC's Passions, FX's the Shield, Comedy Central, the Young And The Restless, fifty-plus songs for various MTV shows, and many more television and cable placements here and there along the way. I've had video game placement in the NHL and Triple Play series, Alice in Wonderland, James Bond, The Sims, several SONY games, Guitar Hero, and a smattering of other games on many different platforms. I've composed music for national and regional ad campaigns including Nissan, HP, Microsoft, plus countless other corporate gigs and scores of independent films that you may or may not have seen. The complete list goes a long way and I'll spare you the details. Scan the link below to see more of them. In addition, I record and produce local artists- I've recorded hundreds of albums and EP's in my eighteen years of running a commercial recording studio.

Complete credit list:

So now you're beginning to get the gist of what I do. I work for a living doing music, not on a grand scale, but I'm making a life of music. This book is about how you can do what I do at the level that I do it. I wear a lot of hats to make it all happen and no two days are ever the same. Surviving in this business is often about having and maintaining friendships and connections, sometimes finding the right niche market, and almost always embracing a willingness to collaborate. While I may not be a household name in the music biz, I don't have to worry about the paparazzi.

What information could I have to offer someone who is just starting out or simply wants to further their own career? I'm hoping that by showing you how I've used the resources I had to get to where I am today, perhaps you'll be able to discover something that might further your success in music.

Part I: My path to Stardom… sort of…

The Emmys

When you think of the Emmy Awards show, you picture the event you see on TV with the red carpet, the famous Hollywood Stars, the exorbitant outfits, the flash of the cameras, and you think, "Wow, I'm *so* far away from that world." I wanted to start this book by talking about the Emmys because I'm immediately going to dispel some magic here. As it turns out, not only do the Emmys salute those who have achieved a nationwide celebrity status, the Emmys also give out awards for local programming as well. This "local programming" element is where things get very interesting. Winning such a prestigious award suddenly becomes much more accessible, much more possible, because you only have to compete on a "local" scale.

There are nineteen Emmy chapters across the United States. When I won my most recent award back in June of 2012, the San Francisco Emmy chapter awards ceremony had fifty-nine categories. This includes an area from Hawaii, Nevada, and up to Oregon. Fifty-nine categories is still a lot of competition when you're talking about an area as large and ethnically diverse as the San Francisco Bay Area and beyond, but consider this: several awards went to both Spanish and English recipients, so altogether there were *ninety-two* Emmy awards handed out that night. Often there would be a team of 5 or 6 people who worked on the project- people like the director, the cinematographer, the editor, ahem... hopefully the music guy, and everyone received his or her own engraved Emmy. There must have been 150 awards handed out the evening of the awards show. So when you multiply 150 trophies by nineteen Emmy chapters, one begins to realize there are literally thousands of Emmy awards given out across the United States each year.

Here's a surprise: the Emmys is a business. Let me reiterate. The Emmys, just like a restaurant, a frame shop, or an insurance franchise, is a business. And just like any other awards show or any other company, it needs to make money. There's only one catch to winning an Emmy: one has to be a member. What does it take to be a member of such an exclusive club? What possible qualifications must one possess to be able to be included as part of this enlightened circle? It's pretty easy, really. If you can come up with 100 bucks, you can join. Seriously, that's it! One doesn't have to have a track record, a long history of being in the biz, or have had anything air on TV. Renewing a membership for each subsequent year is only $65! Of course, there's no real reason to enter unless you've been a part of something that has actually aired. If you've worked on a project that may be worthy of at least entering, you also have to fork over $65 per category that you submit.

Perhaps one of the best-kept secrets is that just about everything professional that gets entered has a high chance of getting nominated. This is *huge*. It isn't hard to get nominated. The man who runs the Northern California Chapter once asked me if I would judge some entries from the Heartland Chapter in Colorado. Judging was fun and easy. There was a very simple on-line form with radio-style buttons and a point system for every entry. Most of the spots I watched were great and totally professional. These candidates understood what it takes to make something look and sound great. Of course there were a few other entries that left me wondering why they thought it was worthwhile spending the entry fee money. Unless I was just missing something, these entries were about as amateur as they could be and definitely not worthy of a professional award. I made my notes and wrote down my recommendations. I'm sure I wasn't the only one judging this chapter. There are supposed to be at least five judges, and I'm sure the Emmy organization has no problem getting enough certified peers to make recommendations.

Maybe it's luck, but almost every thing I've entered thus far into the Emmys (14 out of 16 entries) has at least earned a nomination. There were two entries that didn't get a nomination for 2013. Both spots looked great, and I honestly don't know why they didn't get a nomination. Oh well, can't win 'em all!

Once you have an Emmy nomination, you'll want to go to the awards show, which costs around $100 per ticket to attend. Most people bring someone special with them, so chances are you're in for two hundred dollars for the show itself. Adding it all up, between the $100 cost of membership, the sixty-five dollar entry fee, (I entered in two categories my first year, so my entry fee was $130) the cost of going to the awards show, they made a tidy $430 just from me. At least a nice dinner and some entertainment was provided at the black tie event.

The cool thing is that they also want you to win so you'll come back the next year. So they have a lot of categories, and they give out an abundance of awards.

As I was saying, a large percentage of the higher quality material that gets entered gets nominated. All you have to do to enter one of these regional chapter Emmys is have something that airs *only* locally. That's right. Something that airs on a nationwide basis can't really qualify for one of these area wide Emmy Awards, although there are some exceptions. They no longer offer a specific music category at my chapter, but there were still 58 *other* categories for 2012 where they handed out awards, and every one of those pieces needed music. Think about visual media. Everything you see on TV needs music, with the possible exception of the stopwatch on 60 Minutes. I'll say that again: everything you see on TV needs music. Here's another one for you. Audio without video is radio, video without audio is... technical difficulties. Spots which feature specifically composed music are typically going to sound better, look better, thus *be* better than the spots using stock music added on as an afterthought. Chances are that no TV show or no director with a tight budget is going to actually pay for a composer unless they think it's well worth it to do so. If the spot looks great but the canned music they added isn't helping, the spot will definitely suffer, until the director gets smart and hires a composer to bring the spot to life.

The Grammys have a few similarities, but the big difference is that they don't have the advantage of having accessible regional awards. So if you ever get nominated for a Grammy, you're really doing something amazing. Just like the Emmys, the Grammys costs $100 per year to become a voting member, and going to the awards show is around the same cost. To become a voting member, you have to be able to prove that you've been a part of at least six physical CD releases, or twelve on-line releases. If you've spent any time recording a few bands, you may have enough to qualify already. Seriously, it's fairly easy to get to at least this point. There are two great things about being a voting member. One is that you get to vote in the Grammys. You get a secret ballot, and you can vote for as many or as few musicians as you like. There's no secret society here, it's just a bunch of full and part time musicians picking their favorite band. Whoever gets the most votes wins the day. The other nice thing about being a voting member is that you get to nominate anyone's work, even if the nominee isn't a Grammy member! You can suggest some of your own clients for consideration. You can even nominate yourself. Whoever you recommend will show up in the long list of first-round ballots to determine who is nominated. A few months later the final-round ballots are sent to the voting members. Lastly, the winners are announced on the televised broadcast each February.

Here's how I got involved with the Emmys. I am a partner in a music production company called popTuna (more about that later). In 2000, we placed an ad in a publication called the Reel Directory, which is a book listing of all the film and video people in the Bay Area.

The Reel Directory

This publication lists all the people who are involved in film and video. Directors, actors, craft food service people, music and sound designers are all listed. It's so comprehensive that it also includes the pilot who flies the helicopter for aerial shots!

The one and only call we ever got from placing this ad was from a person who needed a version of "The 12 days of Christmas" for an upcoming commercial. He was working at the now defunct TV channel "Tech TV", and the spot was for the equally as defunct electronics store "Circuit City". We recorded our upbeat version of the song, and the music we handed in was approved several days in advance of the production deadline. On the day of the shoot, the actor was flown in, he sang his lines at my studio, and then they shot the commercial that night on location in an actual Circuit City store.

Circuit City Commercial

There was a tremendous amount of pressure riding on us to make the full mix with the vocals happen very fast, so I think we earned a lot of respect from the director. The big payoff came later. We finished that commercial, we got paid, and went to the next gig!

PopTuna sends out email updates every so often (as you should too), and we kept in touch with the director.

After a few years we got a call from the director of the Circuit City spot. He landed a new job in the promotions department at the local CBS TV station and he needed some music for a few upcoming commercials. We ended up doing two spots for him over the next few months. On one song we had a hip hop groove and the spot showed people on the street singing the hook "44 Cable 12", and then we did a promotional spot for a local TV show called "Eye on the Bay" where we hired a few horn players and recorded a dub version of "The odd Couple."

Odd Couple and Station Image spots

The spots went well, the people singing on the street were a big hit, and thrill of all thrills, I got to see my work actually air on TV! The gig went well, and again, we got paid. No big deal, and we were on to the next job.

A few months after the last commercial wrapped up, I received an email from the director. They were going to enter the two spots we did in the Emmys, and he wanted to know if I would like to be a part of that process. My jaw hit the floor. Keep in mind I was where you were about ten minutes ago. I had no idea the Emmys were so accessible. It never would have occurred to me to enter something like this. Don't get me wrong. We knew the two spots we did were perfectly fine, but were they really the best in Northern California? Lucasfilm- one of the biggest, baddest, most powerful film production companies in world is out here- I can't compete with these kinds of multi-billion dollar facilities, who was I kidding? After I picked my jaw off the floor, I paid my membership fees, paid for my part of the entry, and rented a tux. With the tuxedo rental, I had spent somewhere around $530. Sure enough, the spots were nominated, and on the evening of the awards show they both won! Wow, twelve years after making my living completely from music I had finally won some real recognition. It was a proud moment for me and those around me!

Back to reality, even if neither of our entries won that night we could still say we were *nominated* for an Emmy. That's really the whole point, which is being able to put a household word like Award, Emmy, or CBS next to your name in order to bring your name up to the level where people at least feel comfortable hiring you. Even if you're just *nominated* for an Emmy, all people see is Emmy. And if you're in the music biz, all people will *think* is Grammy. Even if nothing we entered made it as far as being nominated, I still could have said that I did a gig for CBS. Your credit list could be something as simple as this:

Your Name Here   CBS

See how impressive that looks having something like CBS next to a name? Suddenly your name is on par with something as big as a major television network. It looks like you're the "go-to guy" whenever CBS needs something done right. Use this kind of leverage whenever you can. Don't be annoying about it, but name-drop on your websites, the back of your business card, your YouTube site, Facebook, etc. You know the drill. Your on-line presence is really one of the few places where you can unashamedly toot your own horn.

So how do you get one of these gigs where you can write music for TV on a local level? You can get in contact with your local

TV station and find the right person to talk to about doing music for their productions. Maybe you know someone who works there already. You can simply ask for the gig, saying something like "hire me to do some music, and let's win some awards!"

They're going to be much more likely to shell out money for a composer if they think there might be something in it for them. In reality very few TV stations are going to spring for a composer, there's just not much of a budget these days. But you can intern at a station, get your foot in the door, and get established. Once you're there for a while, you'll get to know who to talk to. There's inevitably going to come a time when something is being produced in-house and it will need some music immediately! If you're around and can churn out something fast and good, or at least good *enough* when they need it, they're going to trust you the next time. Once you have their trust, they won't risk working with anyone else. After all, their jobs are on the line with every project they do. I hate to sound overdramatic here, but you know what they say about performing artists: you're only as good as your last show. You constantly have to outdo yourself, which makes us grow and learn new things.

Due to either declining budgets, an overuse of library music, or just a reluctance of TV stations to spring for a composer, popTuna has consistently been the only group of composers represented at the Emmy Awards for the entire Northern California Chapter. Being in this minority has given us a real edge over the competition, and winning 6 awards in 4 years is a pretty darn good ratio. My partner and I won 11 Emmy trophies between us for the work we've accomplished through popTuna.

Let's say you're just starting out. You have no gigs, no credits to your name, and certainly no awards- at least not yet. You need a demo, even if it's just on your YouTube page. Take an existing commercial, a section from a video game, or any trailer you want. Mute the audio and create your own version to use as a demo of what you can do. Be sure to say you replaced the audio for demo purposes, and certainly don't re-sell it for legal reasons. The funny thing is that people will think you were hired to do the audio no matter how often you tell them it's only for demo purposes! Remember that thing about having a household name next to your name? Make it sound great and get it on your website.

Sure, we've all heard about the Emmys and the Grammys, but there is a plethora of awarding organizations just waiting for entries. Some of them include the IMA (the Independent Music Awards) and Just Plain Folks. Do a Google search and see a list of hundreds of smaller awards you can enter and win. Someone has to win one of them. Why not you?

Here's another idea. Create your own awards show. Get a friend to be a judge, you can be the only entry, and congrats- you've won! Give it some title like "The American and Worldwide Association of Recorded Drums", or the AWARD Award for short. Put that next to your name and people will think you've really done something great.

The important thing is to just get some recognizable logo or title that you can put next to your name. You'll be surprised at how little time it takes before you start building up a decent list of recognizable names. Getting something on TV is like a two for one. You're able to list the name of the show plus the name of the Network. Video games are the same. You get to use the name of the game, plus you can say you worked with "insert company name here." The interesting thing about some of the video game companies these days is that along with the titles, the name of the organization often has "rock star" status, too. Use it!

Humble Beginnings

I suppose I should talk about how I got my start in the music business. I don't mean to write out my memoirs. I'm just showing my path in the hopes that our commonality may be relevant to you in some way. I know how boring it can be reading about the minutia of someone else's life, but I'm betting there are a lot of parallels.

I'm sure a lot of people reading this book grew up in a musical family. Not me! OK, my father played a little trumpet in high school, and my mom played a bit of piano. My father has owned and operated a small home production studio since I was born. He didn't record bands, at least not very often. His main business has centered around a syndicated radio program called "The Sound of Texas" that runs mostly on small town stations all across Texas. His name is Tumbleweed Smith, and in his three minute daily show, he interviews fascinating people who, in one way or another, embody the spirit of the Lone Star State. He recently did his 12,000th broadcast. Can you imagine doing 12,000 songs? It takes a lifetime. He started "The Sound of Texas" in the late 60's, and in doing this he has amassed the largest private collection of oral history in the United States.

He drives all over Texas, finding interesting characters, and up until I left for college, he would record these people on a portable reel-to-reel tape recorder. Upon returning to the studio he would then edit the 1/4" tape into a three-minute show. This guy was the master of cutting tape. For him it was fast and easy. Well, at least he made it look easy.

When he would finish with a month's worth of programs, he would copy them on an Ampex duplicator machine. We could make three copies at a time. These machines were the size of two small apartment size refrigerators. When I turned 7 years old, he put me in charge of the duplication of his program for my allowance. It was great, I logged in hours and hours of studio time and I didn't even realize I was doing it "professionally"! I thought every kid did this sort of thing. Can you imagine leaving something as important as duplication to a 7 year old? What was he thinking? But I guess I did OK. We were able to keep the house and both my brother and I went to college.

Before Pro Tools hit the scene, my father got an early version of a digital recorder/editor in 1989 called Sound Tools. It was a two-track editor by a little known company called Digidesign. He was a real early adopter of this kind of technology, and despite its limitations it worked well for him for what he was doing. He wasn't doing a lot of multi-tracked things with tons of overdubs, so it was really all he needed for his show. As soon as he got comfortable with Sound Tools, his tape machines started collecting dust.

My father also taught at the University of Texas for 40 years, he still gives speeches, writes an article syndicated in papers all over Texas and has an advertising agency. The guy wears a lot of hats. This multi-hat-wearing thing was a HUGE influence for me. Both of my parents do a ton of things and are constantly on the go. Most of the time you hear people saying that you have to specialize in something, that you have to find your niche. I even said at the top of this book that you sometimes have to find a niche *market*. While I think this is good advice for most people, being a specialist just hasn't worked for me at all. Nor has it been the case for most people I know who are working in this field. I do a variety of different things in the audio world, but I'll get to that later. I may yet specialize in something, but for now, this idea of diversification seems to be my course.

Another big part of my growing up was a three-year stretch from first through third grade where I took piano lessons. In other words I got to where I could play the easy piano version of Star Wars and when I turned fourteen I started playing guitar. Fourteen is a bit late to start on your principle instrument, but I think the piano helped tremendously. Plus, I was absolutely hooked with guitar all through high school. I played a lot of Rush, Iron Maiden, and Ozzy Ozbourne (specifically the Randy Rhodes era). In high school I played in a few rock bands, and I even got to sit in on a few club sessions with some older musicians. (I mean, how else are you going to get into a bar at age 16?) I also started to play a lot of classical guitar. Even back then, I liked the technical side of things. Also in High School I got a job at the local music store on Saturdays, and I worked at one of the movie theatres during weekday evenings. It's funny how after all these years I'm still doing music and film.

Another big asset I had were the friendships I made growing up. I lived in a small town in West Texas from birth all the way until High School graduation, and I had the same close friends throughout that entire time. Some of my friends' parents even went to high school together, so our roots run pretty deep. These friendships will come back in a big way.

When I was a junior in high school, my father interviewed a trumpet player named Dave Hibbard who was starting a commercial music program at a community college in Waco Texas. One of the two-year degrees being offered was recording studio technology. Keep in mind, this was still before Pro Tools, so recording was all done on analog tape and despite the ubiquity of recording schools these days, a place like this was a complete anomaly. The school had an MCI desk and an accompanying MCI 24 track tape machine, a nice mic closet, several pieces of outboard gear, a machine room, a soundproof control room, a huge recording room, the works! We had a great book by Sherman Keene that went through the physics of how sound works, how to align tape machines, suggestions for mic placement, and by the end of the two year program we got to the point where we could run an entire session by ourselves. Besides recording technology, we also had to take music theory, sight singing and ear training, vocal lessons (if you heard me sing you might wonder if they had a money back policy), required attendance at recitals, and instrument lessons in jazz, classical, and country guitar. I was in heaven!

One cool thing that my instructor did was that he had us write down a five-year plan for our goals. I was eighteen, so how could I really think past next week? Goals? Isn't that something that happens in soccer? We could write down anything we wanted to do with our lives, and I wrote down that I wanted to start a recording studio. At the time I didn't think it would ever happen, especially given the historical perspective of the expense of purchasing large "couch-sized" studio gear. Anything recording-wise at this point in time involved a huge mixing board, an expensive tape machine, outboard gear... forget it! There was no way that owning a studio like that could financially happen for me at that time, but I obviously *wanted* to do it.

During that two-year recording program, I also started a cover band, and eventually we were playing all over Texas and Louisiana while we on vacation from school. Soon I was able to pay my way through school and pay most of my living expenses just by playing in a band. Man, I thought this was great!

The reason I'm bringing up the cover band here was the realization that we often had to "think outside the box" to create our own opportunities for gigs. We talked to the cafeteria department on campus about starting a Friday lunch band series where people might actually eat in the cafeteria for once and listen to a band while they ate. That idea went off fairly well, and as far as I know that program is still going on today. That success prompted us to approach a local restaurant about starting a "Tuesday Student Night" where some of the other bands from school could play. Another example was that our bass player had a girlfriend who was active in the community, and she would have us play at events that might not normally pay for live music. We would play at places like Chamber of Commerce banquets and small local festivals. Sure, we had lots of regular bar gigs just like any other band, but sometimes you have to be creative about getting work, and being in this band was a big eye opener for that concept. Oftentimes the difference between making your rent payment and... well... not making your rent can be one of these "extra" gigs.

The band had a lot of gear. We would show up to these gigs with our big truck driven by our bass player and another car to carry around the other four of us. We had a big PA that the band shared that was in flight cases; we had keyboards, guitars, a drum kit or two, amps, mics, cables, and luggage for the road trips. Think about all the money that we put into learning how to play these instruments, and compare that to the fact that frequently we would only make one hundred dollars a night. Yeesh. More often than I would like to admit we would have to split that one hundred dollars between five people.

After a few years of this I understandably got to a place where I decided there was simply no money in music. Yes, I was able to support myself, but just barely. Well, there was that three day stretch where there wasn't anything to eat, but that's another story. I guess that's one place where the recording school didn't put a whole lot of emphasis- actually making money in the music biz. There's money- a lot of money- to be made out there, I just didn't know where to find it. In another turn for the weird, the school's recording classes slowly started to be more about bible study than recording, which didn't seem to fit my personality being a Jewish kid from West Texas. I said enough was enough, and I applied to and got accepted to the University of Texas at Austin as a Mechanical Engineer.

Austin

Austin is a great town for music. It's a very guitar centric town and it feels like everybody plays very well. Even the guy who bagged my groceries was a better guitar player than I'll ever be. When I first moved there, I felt terrible about my decision to leave music. I had feelings like I choose money over my passions, or I had "sold out." In retrospect I was making these choices, and I wasn't happy. About halfway into the semester, I had a dream about my career path that would forever (I hesitate to even say this because it sounds so cliché) change my life.

In the dream, I was in a large office building, running around and doing whatever office people do. (I still don't really know.) A piece of music that I like to play called "Recuerdos de la Alhambra" was booming over the loudspeakers, but only the melody line was playing, thus creating a sense of fragmentation for me. During my haste in the dream, I bumped into a guy with long grey hair who was carrying a stack of papers. The papers fell to the ground and went all over the place. As I was helping him gather them up I realized that the papers he was carrying were manuscript paper with nothing written on them except for the first few pages. When I looked into the guy's face, it was my face. There are a lot of ways to interpret this dream. One is that I've watched the Empire Strikes Back waaay too much, but my take on this is that I have a lot of music to write and a lot of pages to fill. Decades later, every time I start a new song or piece of music that isn't for a client I still think about that dream. After all these years, this dream is my motivation, and it's more motiva-motivational than being paid to create something. It's both a comfort of being able to do music and my fear of not doing it. After experiencing this dream, I realized that I had to go back to music at least in *some* way, and I wasn't going to be truly happy about doing much else.

I don't recommend going into the music business unless you have to, but this dream was my "have to." Think about why you're doing it. It isn't an easy path.

Within days of having that dream, I discovered that a classical guitar program lead by Adam Holzman (an instructor from Miami) was going to start the next fall semester at UT. The bad news was that the registrar said I was too late to apply. The instructor's student load was already booked. When the next semester started I showed up unannounced at Adam's office door with my guitar, and I played him the music that was playing from my dream "Recuerdos de la Alhambra". After hearing me play, he figured out a way to get me in the program. I graduated 4 years later with a BA in Music with classical guitar as my principle instrument.

While I was in school at Austin, I started replying to the "bands seeking musicians" listings in the free local newspaper called the Austin Chronicle. I auditioned with a few musicians and formed a band called "Culture Shock" playing original music. We got to be sort of big fish in the small pond of Austin. We were weekend headliners at a lot of the big clubs in Texas, we played SXSW, we eventually had a manager and a separate booking agent, we had our own lighting guy, sound person, two roadies, and a private rehearsal space. We didn't make any money but at least we broke even. We had a lot of fun, too.

I only mention this band because through this band I was voted as one of the top ten best metal guitarists in Texas in Texas Beat Magazine- right up there with Dimebag Daryl and Ty Tabor of Kings X. You have to understand, I'm a really good guitar player, but so is everybody else in Austin, just ask my grocer. I was very surprised that I was chosen for this award given the incredible talent pool in Austin. Nonetheless, I used that award winning moniker to get other gigs. This was where I learned that all I had to say to open a few doors was that "I was voted as one of the top ten best guitar players in Texas." To get someone's attention I simply needed to convey that I had some success. It got me a very minor endorsement from Hamer guitars. It allowed me to get into a few auditions, it got me another job at a music store and I acquired quite a few students out of winning that award. As much as a popularity contest as it was, it was also a real defining moment for me. It gave me legitimacy about what I was doing musically for myself and for those around me, and I gained confidence for what was coming up next: graduation.

Graduation. The great equalizer. This is where you go from the comfort of school to being in the "big bad world." Graduation can also be thought of as a transition or a new beginning- like when you're leaving a job or moving on to a new chapter in your life. It doesn't matter where you're coming from, any transition is rough, especially if you're going into the music biz. How do you go from doing whatever it was you did before to suddenly working in the music industry? Here's the real disappointment: I have no clue. Wait! Don't put the book down yet! Hang on so you can see how I got to where I am with what was around me. I bet the way you'll make it in this business will be a similar story to mine, and maybe, just maybe, you can apply what I did to your career path.

Want to do filmwork? Make a film!

Remember those friendships I talked about while I was growing up? My core group of friends decided that we needed to do something to keep our relationships alive after college. I have a friend named Jance who was into computers. Remember, this was the pre-internet era. Jance had an Apple Macintosh IICI and was running a program called Vision, a midi sequencing program from a company called Opcode. From his yearlong stint in a metal band in New York, Jance had acquired a power amp and some "nice" speakers (Yamaha NS10-M's), a rack mounted mixer, a synth, a drum machine, a 4 track, and an SM57. With all his gear we felt like we were ready for anything. Ah, 1992 was a great year for consumer technology. We could stripe the 4-track with SMPTE time code via his midi I/O box and have midi synced with the guitars, bass, and vocals via the computer. We even recorded a local band with this set-up. Thank goodness they were very understanding friends of ours and didn't expect too much. We learned a lot from the experience and had a great time.

After about 6 months with this set-up, Vision became Studio Vision. Now it was possible to record two tracks of audio on the computer if you had an Audio Media II card from that same small company my father was using called Digidesign. This was big. Huge. Epic. Being able to record digital audio along with our midi stuff on one screen was an enormous leap forward. Plus, we could edit and move the audio clips around in time! We felt like we could really do something.

By the time I graduated college, another friend of ours named Zane was already working in L.A. as an animator. He had a girlfriend who was working as a film producer. Zane had an idea for a script, and he suggested that we should think about making a movie. After all, he had a 16 millimeter Ariflex camera, and making a movie was perhaps the one thing we could do that would pull our talents together. This was purely in the interests of keeping our friendships alive after college.

A third friend of ours named Charlie, who had always liked to take pictures when we were growing up, would become our de-facto cinematographer (when he wasn't working as a nuclear engineer in San Jose). Zane got to work editing his script. Jance and I scraped together what little money we had and bought a shotgun mic and a used DAT player with a portable battery pack. We built a boom for the mic out of a broom handle, a piece of PVC T-pipe, and some rubber bands. We even did a few successful tests to make sure we could stripe time code and sync to the VCR.

We were going to make a movie, and yes, we were nuts.

Our game plan was to move back in with our parents for the prep, hire some actors, and get ready for a two-week shoot back in our hometown. We loaded the car with our computers, DAT recorder, mics, and not much else. Then we made the long drive "home."

The script for the film was a philosophical take on friendship and the afterlife, set as a Western. I'm not kidding. We made a list of all our resources and built the script around the things we knew we could get for free and as it turns out, we had a lot going for us. There was an old family friend who was an eccentric (that means wealthy) rancher in our hometown who had built a castle on his ranch. He offered full run of the place while we shot. The castle was complete with a large medieval banquet hall, secret passages, hidden refrigerators filed with all the Budweiser one could drink, suits of armor, horses and an old time saloon. We had amazing help in terms of period costumes, horses, other locations, equipment, cars, encouragement, and lots of volunteers. It was a dream come true.

Here's the synopsis of the film:

"Past lives. Dead outlaws. Warm beer. All these await Charley Stone in the afterlife, and life after death ain't quite what he expected. Charley is reunited with two old friends: a rifleman named Jake and a philosophizing barkeep, Cole, as well as a band of ruthless enemies from lives past. Somewhere in the harsh drylands lies the keys to Charley's forgotten past- a troubled former life as Ben Kane, a Texas Ranger whose ruthless justice sent many outlaws to Hell long ago. Part action movie, part philosophical musing, Hell is Texas is a gothic western that redefines the ghost story - a harsh tale of redemption, rediscovery, and revenge from beyond the grave".

Was it possible to make this any more unappealing to the masses? What were we thinking? We had never done anything this big. No thirty-second commercials, no documentaries, not even a film short. I mean we had no experience whatsoever. We jumped headlong into doing a feature length film, more or less on a whim.

Did I mention we had no money? We had no idea what we were do-ing, but we did it anyway.

We accidentally did a few smart things along the way. We were willing to collaborate, and we got a ton of help. I'm not talking about the kind of collaboration where you end up not having any con-trol over your project, I'm talking about the kind of collaboration where you get someone who is good at what they do and you let them do it.

We went to Dallas and placed notices on bulletin boards stat-ing we were looking for actors for a film. It wasn't an actual paying gig for the actors. All we could offer was the film credit and poten-tially some back-end points for their effort. Luckily, one of our actors named Tyler Mason was also an aspiring filmmaker, so he knew ex-actly what he was getting into. He had a ton of politely offered and well-placed suggestions during filming. Another one of our actors, Mark Nutter, was also a great talent, and both performers went on to make a living as professional actors, both in L.A. and in Texas. I like to think their success was partly because they were able to have a star-ring role in a feature film in their credit list. Who am I kidding? I'm sure they would have made even it without us.

Another good example of collaboration was when we con-vinced Ron Hubard and Janet Hurley, a team of fight choreographers, to help us out. We had no idea what to do in terms of blocking out a fight scene so we gave them the opportunity to do whatever they wanted within the parameters of the script. They were chomping at the bit to be able to have some creative input within the scope of a feature length film, and both Dave and Janet needed some demo reel material even more than they needed the money. It turned out to be a good fit. The couple had a few recommendations for some additional help in the form of a stunt man named Jamie Dierlam, a pyrotechnics expert named Randy Moore, and a special effects make-up guy named Dave Whitley. All arrived on location for a one week shoot for free. Amazing! We would have been lost without this talent pool. All we had to do was let these guys do what they were born to do. Here's a secret: Zane was so nervous about asking these guys to work for free that he threw up after our initial lunch meeting with these guys. We knew nothing would have happened if we weren't willing to work to-gether so we plowed ahead. Sure, we also gave up a few back-end points, but you can't get something for nothing, and we knew we would have to offer something on the back-end if this film was to be-come a reality. We also fed everyone very well while on location. We learned that lesson very early on, and it's something every parent knows. If you want something to go well, then have a lot of food and snacks on-hand. Cranky people generally aren't creative people, par-ticularly when they're working for free.

All in all we spent about eight months on the film. It took about four months for pre-production, then the two-week principle photography shoot. When we had the beginnings of a rough cut it revealed how many more pickup shots we needed. We shot the entire project on 16 MM (millimeter), and we rented a silent camera for the two-week shoot when we needed to record dialog. We only used Zane's very noisy 16MM camera for pick-up scenes and slow-motion shots. We were so lucky to have had the ability to live for free with our parents during this time. We were very busy working on the film the entire time we were there and we had a great time during our stay. We also realized it was time to leave before we wore out our very generous welcome.

We packed up our gear, said our goodbyes, and moved in with our cinematographer/Nuclear Engineer friend Charlie in his one bedroom flat in San Jose. Eventually we found a four-bedroom house to rent in a suburb of San Francisco so our poor friend Charlie could finally get some sleep.

Editing and doing post-production was a real education. Zane had all the film transferred to ¾ video tape, and he would give us a VHS copy whenever he made a change to the rough cut. Jance and I would stripe the tape with time code, and get to work with our 40 megabyte hard drive. That's not a misprint. We only had a 40 meg hard drive. That was state of the art for 1993! You can't even fit a high res .wav file on a 40 meg space, much less a film project, but that's what we had to work with. Toss in the fact that we were working on DAT specs (16 bit 48K), and it's a real wonder we made this happen at all. Our solution was to work mostly with MIDI stuff on the music end- MIDI doesn't take up much hard drive space.

Eventually, we spent the big bucks and got a 400 meg hard drive when the technology became available. So while we increased our working space by a factor of ten, our useable working space was still scarcely more than half of a CD! We had to split the film into four sections to get the audio completed. We would finish one section

44

and then back it up on our DAT drive, wipe the drive clean and start on the next section. Oh, we had to write a score and create sound effects, too. Since there was no sync with the camera when we actually filmed, we had to manually line up each segment of digital audio to the video and match it with the cut.

Here's a lesson for you aspiring filmmakers out there: spring for the time code enabled gear. You won't regret it. Luckily, we had very organized notes from the field recordings that we would capture throughout the day. We were constantly recording audio in the field-things like tire squeals, horse sounds, and anything else we could get our mics close to. We kept very careful logs about what sound was on what DAT tape at which time. To fill in any gaps we may need, we sent off for a free demo audio CD from Hollywood Edge that had about 100 sounds. It was just what we needed. I think they still offer free downloads as a demo. I can't believe how many sounds we used from that free CD. You would think that not having access to a comprehensive sound effects library for a film project would be a serious drawback, but it turned out to be OK for us. Most of the sounds we used for the film were things that we recorded ourselves, so they were "one of a kind". These unique sounds add a certain amount of character to the film. While the majority of our sounds were the "real thing" and utterly unique, the trade-off was that for the smoke and mirrors magic that a film project is, sometimes the real thing just isn't hard-hitting enough. We were very happy that the free demo CD had so many useful sound effects to help make up for any missing impact.

Not long after we started working on the first draft of the film, the audio/midi program we used called Studio Vision was able to play back 4 tracks of audio. Those extra two tracks, which doubled our track count, helped our work flow immensely, and soon after we actually got our first rough cut finished.

Incredibly, there was some actual interest in the film. Our producer back in L.A. was doing a great job of scheduling meetings and trying to get it "picked-up," and two companies thought they could do something with it. The distributers wanted to make a lot of changes and we would have had to reshoot a lot of material. They wanted so much new material that it felt like they wanted an entirely different film altogether. Plus, there was very little money involved for us and no money to actually pay for any additional shooting. I think the total they were offering was somewhere around …nothing. With the deep script revisions these distributors were asking for, we felt very uncomfortable working with people who obviously weren't into collaborating with us.

Suffice it to say that the deals were so bad that in the end we decided not to do either one of them. Actually, I can't believe they were even talking about handling it. The film was definitely low budget, but it did have some compelling things going for it. For one, it was an all-digital production in terms of audio, which was a radical thing back in 1993. Given the wacky setting, we thought we could do better than the offers that came in.

Was not taking these offers a good idea? We'll never know. Not surprisingly, we were out of money, we had to get jobs to make ends meet, but we still had our pride. The film literally sat around for a few years until Zane found a job that had some amazing resources to add to the film. We're not talking about the kind of resources that would take it out of the low budget realm, but enough color correction, image stabilization, computer graphics, and other things here and there that really tightened up the cut and stepped up the production value a notch or two. There were enough improvements to the project that we were able to enter it into the Digidance 2000 Digital film Festival, an offshoot of Sundance. From there we landed a deal with a company called North American Films and they agreed to take the film "as-is"! With this deal, the film would be available to buy/rent at video stores, and it would also be available as an impulse purchase at other places like 7 Elevens and other various convenience stores.

OK- we didn't make a meaningful theatrical run, nor did we win any Oscars, but what an accomplishment. We did it with no real money, untested gear and technology, no real experience, and yet it eventually sold. Sometimes you just have to go for it. Nothing will happen if you don't make it happen, and now we have a film to our credit that we made, produced and sold.

Out of Work

While we were waiting for the film to get picked-up, we had to face the reality that we had to find some work. We were living in San Francisco and after having lived in Texas my entire life I was a stranger in a strange land. Outside of my friends, I knew no one in California, absolutely no one. I was one year out of college, broke, and unemployed. I felt if we had finished the film in Austin, I would have had a much better shot at working in one of the many recording studios where I had already worked. I thought because I had some friends in the music department of U.T. who were *already* working in the field, perhaps I could have landed a job in a production house as a co-writer or studio musician. I tried long and hard to find a job at various recording studios and production houses in the Bay Area. I then tried to intern at some of these places, but I could rarely get my foot in the door to work for free, and finding a paying job seemed impossible.

So how do you do it? How do you go from where you are now to working in the music biz? What I like to say here is that there are not a lot of jobs, but there's plenty of work, and some of the work actually pays! I was making the wrong assumption: I was thinking that I could find one gig, a permanent job, and that would be the end of my worries about working in the industry. Some people will get a job placement through their schools and some people will do what I couldn't manage to do, which is to cold call at the right time and place and either get an internship or actually get hired. Hey, it happens to some people, but most of us won't be so lucky. Keep reading. I'll show you how I s-l-o-w-l-y got to where I am now.

Even the part of my job of being a recording engineer isn't that glamorous. I have the kind of job where I do a daily grind working with local artists who, while very talented, aren't quite selling gold or platinum records. Or I'll do a lot of work where maybe I'm not composing for the latest summer blockbuster movie, but I'm creating music for corporate gigs where apart from the people I have direct contact with, I go largely unnoticed by anyone. The important part is: I'm making a living making music. I've essentially done it "under the wire", but I'm making it happen.

Going back to where I was after the film, I had to lower my sights a bit. I got a job at a music store, selling guitars and giving guitar lessons. Oh well, at least it was "kind of" in music. How did I get the guitar lesson part of the job? I used my credits and awards! I had a music degree, and I had won that guitar award a few years back. They *had* to let me teach, right? At least the music store job was somewhat related to music, and it's better than answering phones for "Hair Club for Men" (which I did for a few months before I hustled the music store job).

Eventually, I began to acquire my own gear. I bought an Apple Power Mac 7200/75 (the 75 described the single 75 megahertz processor. I currently have a 12 core 3.2 gigabyte machine), a Roland XP-80 keyboard that I still use today, my own copy of Studio Vision Pro and an Audio Media III card by Digidesign that could play eight tracks of audio instead of four. The card fit into a PCI slot inside the computer. I spent about five grand on my initial gear purchase. Not bad for a guy working minimum wage and teaching on the side.

Mixing anything on that early rig was difficult, not like the plug-in frenzy of today's world. If you wanted to add an effect, like reverb, compression, or even something as simple as EQ, you had to either record it that way or you had to physically patch a cable out of the left output of the Audio media card into the input of the effect, and then from the output of the effect back mono into the right input of the card. Just to make it more difficult, there was no way to monitor the effect while listening to the mix. It required a guess at what the effect might need to be, re-patching the cables back to the card for monitoring and then trying it again. And again. What a hassle! But that was all I could afford at the time, and even that gear was pushing my financial limits. I had very few pieces of gear. I knew them well, and I stretched the technology as far as I could. A little confession here: I knew it was essentially crappy gear. I never pretended otherwise. But it was good *enough* and I never felt too ashamed about the "cutting edge" gear I had.

As long as your gear is "good enough", things are going to be fine. You don't have to work on the latest and greatest version of Pro Tools HDX to deliver high quality recordings. You just have to get good results from the gear you have, even if you're just using free software on a cheap laptop. The things that Avid's M-Box can do would have seemed like magic to us back in mid 90's. If we could make it on crap gear like what we had when we started, imagine what you can do these days. You won't believe what I was able to do with that lousy set-up. Never let your gear hold you back.

Gathering Steam

As I said before, I knew no one in San Francisco and it wasn't like the music store was going to provide any real studio or gigging opportunities for me. If you live in a sizeable town, there are often free newspapers, online forums, or "want-ads" published every week. They often have a "bands seeking musicians" section in it. Just about every small or large town has something similar. I answered a few ads and set up some auditions. I ended up meeting a singer-songwriter named Renee Harcourt. Renee's "claim to fame" was that she had a song chosen by a music supervisor for a show called Melrose Place. Through that audition, we formed a band that played around the San Francisco Bay Area. The band ultimately went nowhere, but I mention this project because through this band we got picked-up by a producer named Jeffery Cohen. Jeffery owned a recording studio in Sausalito called Boomtown.

Boomtown was the home of Keller and Cohen, a music production company that created music for film and TV. Before the session for the band would start, we would sometimes catch Jeffrey on the phone to Mattel toys about a Hot Wheels commercial, or talking to the ad agency Y&R about a Taco Bell ad. Reneé and I thought that this kind of gig would be ideal. Here was a guy, or a small team of people, that did music full time as a *day job*. Wouldn't it be cool to do something like that? Hmmm.

Just as the CD with our producer was coming to a close, our bass player Mona Gnader left the band. She scored a chance to audition for Sammy Hagar, who has been a veteran rocker guitar player for many decades. What a great opportunity for her! She knew one of the musicians in the band and Sammy wanted a female bass player who could sing high harmonies. She got the gig and ran with it.

Reneé, the drummer (Billy Lee Lewis), and I weren't happy with one of the songs we recorded with Jeffery at Boomtown, so we thought we would give my little recording set-up a try. We re-arranged the song and recorded a new version. We totally nailed it at my studio and we had more fun than we ever thought possible in the process of doing music on our own terms. After we finished our second song at my place, we felt like we could do anything we wanted with my set-up. We started a new project and named it "Sugar Danks." We would only do studio recordings and had no intentions to play live. This studio project will come back in a big way. For now, we were just writing for fun and no one was going to tell us what to do or how to sound.

First Studio

Remember my Nuclear Engineer/cinematographer friend Charlie? He was asked to do an in-house video for a new product that GE was making. The video was about a jet stream of water that could cut steel and the higher-ups wanted some "production value" for their video without having to hire an external producer. They say some gigs come from strange places, but a gig like this coming from "Homer Simpson" seemed way out of left field to me, but I wasn't going to complain. I wrote and recorded the music, which helped to get their message across and the muckety-mucks at GE liked it. The product wasn't so successful that today you can find a steel-cutting-jet-streamer at Target or anything, but we got another gig out of it. Then another. Then one of our roommates left. A new roommate was arriving and her living room suite was scheduled to occupy the studio space. Charlie and I decided to split the expenses on a small office space in "The City".

The space we found was in one of the hippest parts of San Francisco. It was on the same block as several live venues like Slims, DNA Lounge and Club Paradise. The space was tiny, just 220 square feet and we furnished it with a video desk (OK, a door placed horizontally over two cinderblock "legs") and a used Omnirax desk for my gear. We built an isolation booth (more like an eye-sore-lation booth) in a corner out of some free office cubicle partitions that I got from a friend. I needed a few things if I was going to continue on my own, so Reneé loaned me her speakers (Yamaha NS-10M's), I bought a CAD Equitek 3000 large diaphragm condenser microphone and purchased a used 16 channel Yamaha ProMix 01 from the music store to replace the mixer that I shared with Jance. The mixer only had two outputs, so I had to premix the signals within the mixer before I hit "tape", but at least now I could more or less record a live kit with the 8 mic pre-amps.

I also needed a name. I've always had a love of numbers, and when I write my signature, it's always looked more like numbers than letters to me. The "B" in my name looks like a one and a three, and the "Z" resembles the number 2, so I called the studio "Studio 132".

I didn't really think too much about it at the time, but this was my first studio. Seriously, my only real thought was: "how can I continue making music, yet not be cramped in a tiny bedroom?" The way I looked at it, establishing the studio was a win-win situation. The worst-case scenario was that no real gigs would ever happen, but my share of the rent was so low that one hundred dollars a month for the space wouldn't kill me financially. I made at least that much and more on the gigs that Charlie was bringing in. Yes, I bought some extra gear, but I would have had to do that anyway if I wanted to continue to record because Jance was moving away. Opening up my own place was a no-brainer. There was no huge investment to keep me up at night. There were no real worries. It was all very simple and natural to "hang a shingle". I unknowingly learned a big lesson about this business, which is to grow *slowly*. Grow your clients, and simultaneously grow the business. Earn more so you can spend more, but put a little in reserve for when you hit a dry spell. I've seen a lot of big studios come and go during the last twenty years in the Bay Area.

They all made the same mistake: they had too few clients to support the infrastructure. As a result, they all faded away when the money ran out. I'm not saying don't put money into the biz, because "it takes money to make money" as they say, but invest wisely.

I had a very low client flow in he beginning. I had the gigs that Charlie was bringing in and then there was the occasional person that came into the music store that needed a karaoke version of a song and could afford to pay me to make it. Sugar Danks was recording in my studio, but there wasn't any money in that yet. So let's take a look at the grand total… that's umm…not very much happening. Oh well, it's all for the love of music anyway, and I'm having a good time, right?

The funny thing is that when you start paying money for re-curring expenses like rent and a phone, your perception starts to change. I now had what is known in the business world as a "going concern", and more and more I found my focus shifting to trying to get people… well, let's just call them clients, in the studio to record. I started to do some of the things you can do for free, like putting up home made flyers at all the music stores and asking people if they knew of anyone who wanted to come in and record.

Digital recording was still a new thing. As far as 1996 is con-cerned, it earned a horrendous reputation as nothing more than a toy for computer programmers. But think about any new technology that comes along: it has to compete with what is already established. Ana-log recording sounded terrible when it first hit the scene way back in 1877 thanks to Edison's phonograph, but after 120 years of experimentation and perfecting, it got to the point where it sounded pretty darn good. Digital had to grow as well, and it will continue to grow. But in 1996 it just hadn't quite developed enough for people to take it seriously.

If you think about the crappy recording gear I had, it's no wonder why people were a bit afraid to pull the trigger to book time at my little studio. But that wasn't going to stop me. I knew what this stuff could do. Just to sweeten the pot, I lowballed my hourly rate just to get a bit of a track record going. I started to run into more and more people who needed audio help, and being a fairly versatile musician, composer, and now a budding professional engineer, I was able to pick up a lot of little gigs for the studio. These were things like converting recordings to cassette tapes, producing accompaniment tracks for vocal performances, and singer-songwriters needing demos. While I had a little bit of work here and there, it still wasn't near enough to be able to quit my job at the music store.

Reneé had a close friend named Monica Pasqual who did a CD at The Annex Studios, just outside of San Francisco in Menlo Park. She worked with a well-known engineer named Tom Carr. The CD sounded great, but she wasn't completely happy with the CD. She was looking for something a bit more modern sounding, and she had some creative differences with her producer, Bruce Khappen, who wanted something a bit more traditional. Looking back, Monica was very young and perhaps couldn't quite articulate what she was looking to do. Reneé's band and I worked with Bruce before we met Jeffrey Cohen, and I found Bruce to be a great producer. He really pulled some things out of me that I didn't think I could do, and I learned a ton from working with him. Bruce has had a great career with David Byrne, Jewel, American Music Club, and is a writer for Recording Magazine. Reneé recommended my studio for some songs that Monica wanted to do. She took the bait, and Monica came in and sang over a piece of instrumental music she had brought in on a DAT tape. All I did was to tell her if something was flat or sharp, or early or late. Other than that I kind of stayed out of the way, and only really volunteered something when asked. When she would ask about something, I had plenty to say. But my restraint helped to get my points across when needed.

Monica just fell in love with the sound we got. Besides, she liked the "vibe" that was happening. With no one telling her what to do, she was finally free to be her own singer, and she really came into her own when we started working together. I should really say that she was free to do her own thing.

This was a huge wake-up call for me. I always thought that a producer was a person who took charge of an artist and dictated exactly what went on in a session. Don't get me wrong. There are producers who are very controlling, and there are times when you NEED to be controlling, but just staying out of the way so the artist can be who they are is essential for most clients, or seems to be, anyway. I've come to find that in order to get the most out of an artist, you have to let them *be* an artist. It's like the people who worked on our film for free: they were happy to do it, and they did their job best when they were given the space to do their own great things. For me, the role of a producer is to listen to what the artist wants to do and turn that into a tangible sonic reality. Let me explain what I mean by a "tangible sonic reality:" when Monica (or insert your client's name here) wants a cool sound, or some cool drum loop, or a guitar, bass, or drum part, you have to make it happen. It's not fair to assume that you have to be able to play every instrument, but for what you are able to play, you have to do it. You may have to fake the rest of it or hire out for the people who actually play the instruments if the budget allows, but it's your job to translate what the artist wants to hear and make it happen. And fast.

Monica and I finished her CD, she got it mastered and we had a great CD release party.

Here's an interesting duality about my production philosophy. I always feel like *I* have to be in total control of what's happening during the session while making the artist feel like *they* are in control. As an example, if you have an idea for something, you need to present it in such a way so that the client thinks it was his or her idea. Let's say the song really needs a vocal part to fill up some "dead air" in a song. Try presenting the part on any instrument you happen to play. Wait for them to suggest that it would sound better as a vocal part. If they're not biting yet, hum it, and then when the light goes on and they want it to be a vocal part, tell them what a great idea that is! Eventually they will feel like everything that happens is their idea, and they'll come back to you again and again because you make then feel so creative. Then they'll start to actually become more and more creative, and less afraid to try their own ideas. Your clients always have plenty of ideas, but getting them comfortable enough to try them in front of you is the real trick.

Here's another one: if they have an idea, and you know it won't work, try it anyway. Let them discover what works and what doesn't work for themselves. Who knows, it might actually work! They'll remember their own mistakes much better when they make them, and at least they won't resent *you* for it. Saying "I told you so" to a client never does much good, but you can always say something like "my fear is that X, Y, and Z may happen if we do this, but let's try it! At least you spoke up about it. When it works, admit that you were surprised. You'll never look bad for taking the "high road."

popTuna

Monica had a friend who was a video editor at a documentary filmmaker's studio called Winton Dupont Films and they needed someone for bookkeeping and phone support. How fantastic is that! Monica had a contact, and this friend eventually pulled her into a job in film. Answering phones and keeping books may not have been *exactly* be the kind of work she wanted, but it got her foot in the door. Monica was no stranger to the world of film and video. She composed the music for a Lego commercial a few years prior, and she wrote for a few film projects when she was in college. After working in that capacity for about a year, Monica talked to Reneé and me about pitching the three of us to do some music for Winton Dupont Films. Her boss, Dave Winton, was directing several shorts for Oprah Winfrey's Oxygen Network. He needed a ton of music, but he abhorred the whole music library experience. There weren't that many fantastic sounding music libraries way back in 1998, and Dave didn't want to waste his time digging through countless pre-packaged "middle of the road" collections of music.

Monica thought that with our combined credit list (her Lego spot and her two albums, the recently completed Sugar Danks CD, the music from "Hell is Texas", and Reneé's song from Melrose place) we could perhaps cast ourselves composing the music for Dave's series. Reneé's day job was as a graphic designer, so she was able to do the artwork for a CD jacket, and now I finally had the excuse to go out and buy the $800 CD burner that I had been eying. We decided to call ourselves popTuna, and when I saw what Reneé had done for the graphics, I simply couldn't believe it. Our credits looked very impressive and we hadn't done anything yet!

Remember when I was talking about putting your name next to a household name to make you look more important? This is what we had:

popTuna

Fox

Melrose Place

Lego

North American Films

As a trio we never did anything together, but we already had an amazing credit list. That was a beautiful thing. We were building on our small successes and making something bigger than anyone of us could have done individually. Ah, the power of collaboration!

We presented our demo CD to Dave, he liked it and we got the gig. The music aired, and popTuna was born.

I have to mention a bit about our workflow. We made an agreement early on that we wouldn't do any work for hire unless it paid *really* well. Once you do a work for hire, you can't ever use that piece of music again. The show (or whoever is represented on the contract) now owns the rights to the music. You wouldn't believe how much stuff we recycle, which we wouldn't be able to do if we didn't own the material. Sure, if we use an old track we typically change the music to fit whatever we're doing. Usually by the time we're finished, the original piece of music is no longer recognizable, but it comes in handy to at least have the legal access to be able to use our old stuff. It also means that a piece of music we composed for a job can still be licensed somewhere else, which will come back in a major way later. I keep a separate folder of the master finals of the music we've composed, and I keep an offline backup of the session and audio files on a different hard drive. Whenever we need something and we don't have the time or the budget to write anything new, we just listen to tracks in the folder of master finals and find something that's already completed, or we look for various ideas or starting points for what might work.

Here's another interesting thing about our workflow. I'm often talking about the power of collaboration, and I'll put my money where my mouth is. The way popTuna works is that we sit in the control room and we come up with parts. We make it happen *together*. This kind of thing would drive most people crazy, including us! It's an interesting way to work in that most composers often work in isolation, yet we're usually doing this together in the same room at the same time. Sometimes Monica comes up with a piano idea, sometimes I write a guitar line, and we respond to what the other is doing, and the piece continues to grow from there. You have to have a real mutual respect for each other to pull this kind of thing off, but we seem to make it happen time and time again. Even after all these years I still feel shy about playing my first response idea with Monica in the room, but as soon as she starts playing in response, it just feels natural.

Little Beast

I'm backtracking here, but shortly after the film "Hell is Texas" was completed, Zane got a job at a place called Western Image Graphics as an animator. It was here that Zane was able to improve the film to the point that it was finally able to be submitted for Digidance. The creative director at Western Image Graphics, Matt Fassberg, was so impressed with Zane (and all of us, really) that the two of them eventually started their own production company called Little Beast when Western Image closed their doors a few years later. Matt has a lot of industry contacts, and Little Beast is often called upon to create some high-end video spots. Little Beast isn't exactly huge: Matt will assemble a team of freelance professionals whenever he lands a big project. The first thing he had me do was the music for Women's World Cup Soccer back in 2000. Then he hired me to create some sound design for the intro video to Electronic Arts' "Alice in Wonderland" video game. For the Alice gig, Matt worked with some people from EA, and when these same guys later needed a freelance sound designer for a new game they were working on, they called me. These contacts led to lots of other work, and with these gigs I can now add a new title to my portfolio of hats I wear in the music biz: Professional Sound Designer.

Little Beast split up after five years, but that turned out to be OK as far as I'm concerned, and it constitutes yet another valuable business lesson. Little Beast's dissolving wasn't the end of my workflow by any means, it just meant that now I had two sources of potential income. Zane moved back to Austin, and he hires me whenever he can. Matt continues to work under Little Beast, and when he needs a composer, a sound designer, or an audio engineer of any sort, he calls me. Remember what happened when Tech TV fell apart? I would never have won an Emmy if that station didn't collapse. Keep in touch with your contacts. They may leave the biz for a while, but chances are they'll need you down the road. If they've trusted your work in the past, why would they hire anyone else?

Industrial Music

What do you do when you don't have any work to do? Just kidding. When you run your own studio you always have work to do, but you also got into this to make music, right? I finally started writing my own stuff. Remember that I have this 'issue" from that dream where I have a lot of manuscript papers fill. Keep in mind I don't sing. At all. This might seem strange coming from a guy who wants to make a living making music. I have a pretty good ear, but I've just never found my voice. OK. I sing a little bit if I have to, but when you work with people who can really sing, you quickly realize that it's better to leave that kind of thing to the professionals. I almost never have ideas for vocal music or lyrics, but I constantly have instrumental ideas, and my favorite pastime is making cool sounds on my computer. I also like very… let's just say … intense music. Since I work with a lot of singer songwriters, it's only natural that I would want to do the polar opposite of what I get paid to do, just in the spirit of shaking things up a bit. So when left to my own devices, the kind of music I'm going to write is typically some heavy instrumental piece with interesting sounds. This will also come back in a very big way.

Sewing The Seeds

As you can see, anything that could remotely be called a success so far for me has been the direct result of a friendship, or at least a friend of a friend through word of mouth. Up to this point I don't think I had any gigs that didn't come from either a friend or someone I met through the music store where I worked. I knew I needed more work if I were to ever leave my day job, and getting to that level seemed like an impossible task. I felt like I just couldn't invest the time or money it would take to completely focus on the studio. I needed more clients, both for popTuna and for the Studio. Right about this time I found out about Taxi.

If you don't already know about it, Taxi gets your music in front of people who need it. It's great for someone like me who has an ability to write and record music but doesn't have very many connections. Here is how it works: Taxi knows someone needing music for something. It could be almost anything, like a record company looking for the next big hit, publishers looking for the next great song, music supervisors needing music for a film or a commercial or a music library looking for music. Whoever's looking for music can run a listing through Taxi. Taxi will post that listing to its sizeable membership and if you as a member think you have something on target for the listing, taxi will listen to your song and decide if it's good enough to forward to the people needing the music. This works out well for the people asking for music. Instead of getting thousands of tracks that they would have to sort through (or not), they get a preselected handful of high quality songs to listen to that Taxi forwards to them. If the company that ran the listing wants to use the music forwarded to them by Taxi, they have to get in touch with the composer directly. Taxi stays out of the deal altogether. Hopefully, you get your material forwarded, and maybe you'll get a phone call.

Placing a listing is free as far as I know. If you want to submit music, it costs two hundred and fifty dollars per year to join, and five dollars for each time you submit a song to a listing. Taxi was started by a record producer named Michael Laskow in 1992. When I joined in 1997, it was still the early days for Taxi and at the time it was sort of a niche market.

There were a few songs by Sugar Danks that seemed like they might be a fit for some of the Taxi listings, so I begrudgingly paid my membership fee and started submitting some songs. I figured I could kiss the time I spent making cassette tapes and entry money goodbye, but what the heck, it was worth trying.

One day, I'm sitting in the studio minding my own business, and the phone rings. It was a music supervisor who wanted to use one of the Sugar Danks songs called "Wide Open" in an independent film about teenage pregnancy called BellyFruit. The music supervisor said she heard my song from a Taxi listing. I was absolutely thrilled! And we got paid $1,000 from the film company to use the song. The best part was that they only wanted to license the music on a non-exclusive basis, which meant that we could use the music on something else should the need arise. That was great. That one call paid for my Taxi membership and the three of us in the band got to split the rest of the money. Cool!

The very next month I got another call from a different music supervisor who wanted to use the same Sugar Danks song in a new film called "The Cure for Boredom". Again, we were paid $1,000 non-exclusively. This Taxi thing was really paying off!

Two months later, I received yet another call from a music supervisor at MTV. MTV! He wanted to use some of the hard-core stuff I was doing for a few episodes of a show called "Real World." Even back in 1998 MTV was already mostly shows.

This really had me wondering what was happening here. Don't get me wrong. I'm grateful for the TV placements and all, but why me? I was still using that same crappy recording set-up, and I was still in that horrible sounding office space where you could hear people in the neighboring offices bleeding in when I turned on the microphone. How could any of this possibly be good enough for MT-f'n-V? In my mind, MTV at the time was the ultimate media machine in that it set the trends, fashion, and culture. I mean, they could have anyone they want playing on these shows, why us? My dream when I was in High School was being on MTV, and I'm sure I wasn't the only American kid with starry eyes. Aren't people killing to get played on that network? Let me bring this back down to reality here. Way back down. No, lower. MTV doesn't pay. While they credit their composers, they pay neither sync fees nor master use fees. You have to let them handle your songs for free if you want them to use it. But if you can get something placed on one of their shows, by all means take it! It'll make more money for you than almost anything else in terms of royalties. They have such deep worldwide penetration and they play the same shows over and over 24/7. They're the most recognized network in the 12-34 demographic IN THE WORLD. They also report their cue sheets to ASCAP and BMI, so the eight cents you get paid in Romania and the penny from the Czech Republic really starts to add up when you consider the entire planet. I'm still making royalties on things that aired more than a decade ago!

OK, so what if MTV doesn't pay *up front*. Why again were they using me and my crappy gear when every other no-name is trying to get in? This is going to sound like I'm meandering here, but hang with me for a minute. Here's a lesson in how to make a good sounding recording. The secret to making a good recording is to get good players playing on good songs. There's very little you can do as an engineer to mess that up. Sugar Danks had some good songs, and we were good players. My gear was acceptable enough, I guess, so that didn't really become too much of a limiting factor. Having these three things will get you very far: good songs, good players, good enough gear. They were enough for us to "rise up" as far as Taxi and MTV were concerned.

Here's another little secret about Taxi. I went to visit them back when they were still in Michael Laskow's apartment in Woodland Hills, Ca. Back then, people would have to send their submissions through snail mail, and the amount of "Santa Clause" size mailbags that would come into their office every week was staggering. The apartment was also crammed with reviewers listening to cassettes and CDs on portable players and making notes as they listened. Then I saw the "outbox". They were using the tiny linen

70

closet in the apartment as the "outbox" for what was to go out to the people who were running the listings. For each listing, there was a little metal tray, and there was hardly anything that was going out. What an eye opener! Taxi won't send anything out unless it's top-tier professional. This told me that the bar is set very high, and if you're getting anything forwarded by the screeners at Taxi, you're doing something right. It's kind of a numbers game, so if you're getting forwarded on a semi regular basis, something will come your way sooner or later. In other words, perhaps the biggest factor in MTV using our music was that we went through the proper channels. Instead of listening to "every other no-name" out there who would for work for "free", they got a small handful of songs to dig through that was pre-screened by someone they trusted. Who knows, the music supervisor at MTV may have signed deals with everyone who was forwarded on that particular Taxi listing. I know they needed a lot of material at the time.

Taxi isn't the only service out there. There's also Broadjam.com, musicsupervisor.com, CD Baby, and pumpaudio.com to name a few. What sets Taxi apart is that they give you very good feedback about your music, which is almost impossible to get from a friend, plus they have a yearly convention that is an amazing networking event.

If you go with Taxi, or something like Taxi, you may get a phone call from someone who's heard only one track they want to use, and apart from the one or two songs that you submitted with the listing, they have no idea who you are or what you do. You have to clue them in to what your skills are. And it works both ways. You have no idea what their needs are unless you ask. For example, suppose the film company calls about a listing they ran looking for dubstep, and in your spare time away from your band you like to write music for banjo. You never know. Just mentioning that you compose this kind of material might trigger them that they are also looking for banjo music for another film, or for the same dubstep/banjo film. Offer to send the music to them, get the address, and send it right away.

Any successful businessperson knows that a customer who has already bought something from you is much more likely to buy from you again. Once they are comfortable working with you, in most cases they will always be willing to listen to some other tracks from you. After all, they called you in the first place, didn't they?

Whatever happens, don't let this new contact fade away. When a stranger calls and wants to use your music that's just sitting around, it's like manna from heaven. These music supervisors and directors are real people who, just like you, are real busy. Time absolutely flies and you will be forgotten if you are not in their face at least every once and a while. Don't be annoying about it, but stay in contact. Email them about what's new in your music. Are you in a band? Put these contacts on your bands' email list. Have you had another placement somewhere? Let them know about it. Create a buzz or a sense of urgency where they feel it's important that they get a chance to use your music before anyone else does, or before you get so famous they can no longer afford you.

It's all about leveraging your successes and building up your credit list so that people feel so confident about you that they know you'll do the job and do it well.

Remember that music supervisor that wanted to use the Sugar Danks song for "Bellyfruit"? I kept in touch with them and was able to visit them in person. They wanted to start a publishing company, and with their contacts they could pitch the music I recorded with Sugar Danks, the popTuna library, my own hard core music, and Monica's CD for various film and TV projects. They wanted to represent *me*, which is funny because except for my hardcore industrial stuff, everything else I did was a collaborative effort. I signed a Publishing Administration deal with Media Creature Publishing, and in the process I was able to include all my music-writing friends, too. It's not like we get a ton of work from this deal, but at least a few times every year they license a piece of music from me or at least one of us anyway. Perhaps the greatest deal from this agreement up to this point was that they placed four of my industrial songs in a series of Nissan Commercials in 2002. My cut was $12,000.00… for each spot. OK, one of them only paid $6,000.00, but still, this became the down payment for my first house. If you know anything about real estate values in the Bay Area, then you know this was a very substantial deal, especially for an unknown musician. Isn't there some joke about the difference between a musician and a large Pizza? A Pizza can feed a family of four. Move over Pizza!

I was one of the early success stories for Taxi, and they ran a print ad with a small interview with me in several magazines for many years.

Taxi ad

Next Steps

This was getting ridiculous. I had to upgrade my gear. I was proud of what I was able to accomplish with that tiny rig, but it was definitely time to move on. Around this time I was promoted to head of the sheet music department, still making most of my living at the music store. I generally only invested in the studio whenever I made extra cash from studio work or popTuna. Beyond my initial $5,000 investment in gear, I almost never put money into the studio with the income from the music store. I needed that to survive. With a bit more work coming in and with some of the Taxi placement money, I bought a real mixer- the Yamaha 02R, a real top of the line Pro Tools rig, some better speakers to go along with my NS10-Ms, and a few more odds and ends. Plus with an actual Pro Tools setup I could finally use plug-ins and change a sound *while the song was playing*! Mixing became such a joy.

Wouldn't you know it. Just as soon as I spent all my extra cash on gear, I also lost my job at the music store. Corporate headquarters decided to pull the funding on the sheet music department, and I could no longer order more printed music to sell for the store. As you might expect, sheet music sales began to decline, and it wasn't long before they made the manager dispose of the sheet music position altogether. That was a huge lesson about a poorly run corporation. The bottom line is king, even if hurts them in the long run. Sure, it hurt me personally for a while. It hurts getting the axe. The manager obviously didn't want me to go, but...

What a gift. Nothing invigorates a business like *having* to succeed. My father also started his radio show when he got fired from a news job way back in 1968. The good news is that the manager of the music store let me stay on as a guitar instructor to ease the transition. I love to teach, and I stayed with the store for a few more years until I just couldn't afford to do it anymore. I eventually made too much money at the studio to commit the time required for teaching.

Studio 132 version 2.0

Holy cow this was scary! I was truly on my own doing music full time without the safety net of a day job. As you can see, it was a long slow road with step-by-step incremental growth, but I still had a long way to go. I was surviving in the biz, but I wasn't making much of a living. Being thrown into having to rely almost exclusively on the studio for an income wasn't exactly ideal.

After coasting along for about a year, slowly building up business, I learned that my building was going to close for a seismic upgrade, and I had four months to get out. This was right in the middle of the dotcom bubble in 2000, and office space in San Francisco, a.k.a. "The Silicone Valley", was running at a 97% occupancy rate, and real estate was some of the most expensive in the country. There were a few recording studios in the area that had closed their doors and were for sale, but they were ridiculously out of my budget. Like who needs 20,000 square feet for $25k per month?

I was determined to build my own space. I managed to find a 600 square foot basement space in a building between Mission and 5th street in downtown San Francisco. It had a sturdy cement floor, and I figured I could make it work. The location had some promise- it was a block and a half away from The Metreon (the most high tech shopping district in the city), and yet a half block away from some of the best crack in town.

To help build the studio, I hired Chips Davis, the acoustical architect who helped to design Skywalker Ranch, to help me plan the facility. That just amazes me. Here's a guy that designed one of the worlds' most premier recording complexes, and yet he's still available to help out the little guys. He wasn't very expensive either. He took some physical and acoustical measurements of the space and gave me a four hour crash course in constructing a studio, including how to build the walls with three layers of sheetrock, how to build the window into the studio room, how big to make the control room, where to put the desk, how to treat the walls, basically everything you can think of to make it possible for me to build out a useable space.

I took excellent notes.

It wasn't huge, but the design included a 14X17 recording room, a 4x4 vocal booth, and an 11X14 control room, and it was all more or less soundproof. Plus, I could advertise the fact that I hired Chips Davis, the architect who designed Skywalker Ranch.

All I had to do was buy the wood and sheetrock, haul it downstairs, and then build it. I've never built anything before in my life with, you know, tools and stuff. A friend of mine gave me a book about construction, plus I had the notes from Chips. I convinced my friends to help me haul down all the wood and 100 sheets of eighty pound, 5/8 inch thick 4X8 sheetrock, and I got to work building out the studio. Building materials and buying lunches for my friends who helped out cost me right around $8000.00. Not so bad when you think about it. That didn't cost much more than my first Pro Tools rig.

When the studio was finished, I was finally able to record with fantastic isolation. Being able to listen to the sound of a kick or snare drum live *without* having to record it and later play it back seemed like an absolute miracle. Why didn't I do this sooner! A friend of mine let me have her Pro Tools I/O box, the 888 24, so I was able to record sixteen tracks at once instead of just eight. I even figured out a way to get six discrete headphone mixes for live sessions out of my mixer, so with a good sounding room and virtually perfect isolation, I started to get a lot more bands coming in to record. Sixteen tracks are usually plenty for basics, eight just won't cut it. Thirty-two, which is what I'm working with now, is better still.

I'm so spoiled. I used to have to settle for recording no more than two tracks at a time. I think now I can theoretically play back 256 tracks through 24 physical inputs/outputs. I've come a long way, baby.

Growing Up

I recently saw a documentary called "Jiro Dreams of Sushi." It's about a sushi chef in Japan. OK, *the* Sushi chef. He is perhaps the greatest sushi chef ever. The documentary talks about his total lifelong dedication to his craft. I mean total dedication. He worked so hard and so intently to the point where his kids often wouldn't recognize him. I was becoming like Jiro- minus the sushi part. I love doing what I do, and I wouldn't trade it for anything, but there some other things in life I wanted to do. It was the year 2001, I was thirty-three years old, and I was completely obsessed with music so much so that I wasn't really dating or going out very much. I'm more or less doing music every waking moment with a laser-like focus. What kind of person will I become if I continue like this? Do I really want to be someone like Jiro? To make a long story short, I found a special someone, and when the Nissan commercials hit, we bought a house and got married. You may be saying, "Don't do it BZ! You're in your prime! Don't stop now!" Things are changing, but they're far from over...

The MixPack

As the internet became more robust, I found that more and more I was sending files through the web instead of delivering a project on CD. There were even a few times when a client in another state would send me some tracks they recorded at home to be mixed. I polished the songs and uploaded the finished master back to the client. Even though the client was never physically at the studio, I was still able to give them a finished mix.

This gave me a great idea. I could start an online service where artists could record in the comfort of their own home, upload the files to a professional studio to mix, and then they could download their finished and mastered mix. The only problem was that I was afraid that I didn't have much of a "track record" of famous bands I've worked with. How could I attract enough customers for an online mixing business without these big names?

At this point, I was living in bedroom community with my wife and our first of two children. A lot of people think that when you have kids, your creative life is over, at least for a little while. It's certainly true that having kids transforms your old life. When we had our first child, we were still a cool couple with a kid, and we still got invited to some parties here and there. Sometimes we could actually go to some of these parties! When we had our second child, it seemed like we stopped getting invited to *anything* anymore. Gradually, our criteria for friendship more and more became based around being with other couples with similarly aged kids.

A neighbor told me about a nearby family with a similar configuration as mine, and the father had a studio in a converted basement just a few doors down from my house. I was told that I should introduce myself and say hello. I'm always a bit skeptical when someone talks about a home studio. I was picturing an M-Box with maybe a small midi controller, and maybe a nice mic or two. So I did the neighborly thing. I knocked on his door and said "hi". I was shocked to find out that not only was Marc Senasac a long time and established career professional engineer, but his newly constructed home based studio was also very impressive, boasting a large format console with racks of outboard gear and a nice Pro Tools HD rig. Marc had a mixed a number of well known artists like En Vogue, The Beach Boys, 2Pac, Tony Toni Tone, and Blue Oyster Cult just to name a few. Our families really clicked and we started hanging out. As you might expect, our conversations often turn toward the geeky side of music.

I started to talk to Marc about my ideas for an online mixing service, and he was already thinking about a similar plan. He pointed me to some websites that were already doing something similar. Darn! So much for being an original. Perhaps there was a way to join forces. What he could bring to the table was his impressive list of acclaimed bands, and the "star power" I could bring to the table was all the corporate work that popTuna was doing plus my film and TV placements. We figured we could make a fairly impressive client list by combining our credits. Sound like a familiar story? Three cheers for the power of collaboration! We decided to call the new service The MixPack. The demand isn't very high, but it more than pays for itself. Sometimes it actually makes some money, but overall it's a way to expand our client list. If you have a physical studio, you're geographically bound to the limitations of clients who can drive to you. If you offer your service on the web, you've just made it possible so that the entire planet can work with you. In reality, it's just a marketing arm of the studio to make it possible to get more gigs, and it allows us to work with people all over the world.

Soon after we started The MixPack, my wife and I had another son, and our little house we shared was clearly not going to be big enough for all four of us. Luckily, we found a house in a less expensive part of the Bay Area in Oakland that was big enough to accommodate the studio and all of our living needs. All I had to do was build another studio. If you have to be a musician *and* be a family man, yet somehow be able to do them both well, it helps if you can cut down on your commute times. All I have to do to go to work is to go downstairs. It's ideal because I can do more of both my work and family duties, and I can't imagine how I managed to get anything done before. Even though we now have a much larger home than before, we pay about the same if you include the amount we were paying for a mortgage on the expensive peninsula plus what I was paying for rent at the downtown location.

Here's the ironic thing about being a family guy. I never had so much work when I was a single guy, and I certainly never had any Emmys until we had kids.

Now that I'm in the new house and new studio, I wear a lot of hats, and I have a lot of ways I can make an income with music. I can produce and engineer, play as a session musician, fix an artists' vocals with AutoTune or Melodyne. I can teach, record an entire band live with great isolation and with discrete headphone mixes, I can master a CD, I'm able to play live, I sell a few CDs of original material, I have a lot of success with my publishers and Taxi, popTuna keeps me busy, I'm featured as a guest lecturer at universities and recording schools, and the MixPack brings in new work here and there. I feel like I'm in my prime, and I can take on anything. Of course, it's taken me 20 years to get here. I remember playing guitar at a show once, and someone came up to me and said, "I would give anything to play like you". I replied, "how about 20 years of hard work, practice and dedication?"

Part II: Tips and Tricks of the Trade

Stayin' Alive

But how do you stay afloat? How do you get the word out about your studio?

I used to advertise in the Yellow Pages, The Guardian, the SF Weekly, and several other local magazines or newspapers that have come and gone. Back in the 2000's, print media was everything you ever needed to handle all your advertising. It seemed like all the local bands read the Guardian or the (insert-your-local-paper's-name here), and it made sense to spend the ad budget there. I would place an ad and new people would call. Simple. But as the internet has grown and become more and more embedded in our lives, print media, at least in terms of advertising for a recording studio, has become virtually obsolete.

When prospective clients call me to inquire about studio time, I always ask how they heard about my studio. Usually, it's by word of mouth, like a friend of a friend or something. If it's not word of mouth, somewhere around 2004 the answer was always Google or Yahoo, and eventually just Google. Google has a deal where you can bid on "adwords" on their search line. The more money you bid, the higher your ad will show on the right hand side of a search, and the belief is that the majority of people will go with the first few ads they see. Then, if they actually click on the ad, they get directed to your site and then they can read about all the wonderful things you've done and hopefully give you a call. Google charges every time someone clicks on your display ad. You have to be smart about using this kind of advertising because it can get very expensive very fast. Some of the words or phrases you can bid on cost upwards of one or two dollars every time a potential client clicks on your ad, so unless you put a limit on how much you want to spend each day, things could get out of control. The hope here is that the more people click on your ad, the more business you'll get.

An even better way to use Google is to get your site to show up organically on the main search results page without depending solely on expensive adword terms. There are some great resources on the web about encoding basic Search Engine Optimazation (SEO) features into your site so that you rank high with search terms like "Recording Studio" when someone in your town looks for a place to record. If this seems too hard or too time intensive to program into your site, believe me, there's a million services that will do this for you. Be sure to get reviews before you hire someone. You want to make sure they know what they're doing! Update your website often and keep it current. If *I* can become my own Web IT guy, anybody can. When I set up my first website, I traded a graphic designer/client a song for the website design, and whenever I need to update things, I go to my FTP site and make changes myself with Text Edit. Even when I do any correspondence through email or Facebook, I'll almost always add the code so that my info is clickable and is relevant to my site. You need to make it easy to bring people to visit your web page.

Remember my success with Taxi? Occasionally, Michael asks me to write an article for his monthly newsletter. I always include a link back to my site at the end of the article. This innocent little link, along with other links from other websites that point back to me, helps my site to rank higher with Google, plus it often leads to new business. Seeing my name as a writer of an article can make someone who has been on the fence about working with me feel much better about moving forward. Find a site that might have some potential clients as members, like a songwriting site, blog, or discussion group that's fairly popular, and ask if you can write as a guest. Or post on a forum with a link to your site in the signature.

Web sites like Facebook, Pandora, or ReverbNation are a great new technology. You can do a search for bands within any radius of a zip code, and then send a message about how you like their music and ask for a way to work together. If you're starting out a studio and just want to build up a client list, tell them that you're just starting out and you'll do one song for free. You'll get a lot of people to respond. When they see how well you do things, they'll come back to you because they'll be happy with your work, and now they'll be happy to pay. They just won't trust anyone else. Ex'pression College, a highly successful recording school in Emeryville, has a program where a band can record for free as long as they're willing to let the students do the recording and mixing. They have no problem filling their students' calendar. The band gets a free recording, the students get a bit of experience, and I bet the students often find work down the road with the bands they record.

Speaking of recording for free, you can also sponsor a "Battle of the Bands" competition. While the idea of working for "free" might not spark much excitement, it's a very profitable thing to do. Here's how I usually work it. Most "Battle" shows involve the winner getting an amount (let's say 20 hours) of studio time, or the winning band can opt to take a cash prize instead (let's say $500.00). If they go for the studio time, the sponsoring studio gets the money. That's you. I know what you're thinking: getting paid $25 per hour won't really pay for that operation your Aunt needs, but almost every band that wins the contest will buy more time. No matter how much you explain how long the recording process takes, all the band can see is the 20-hour block of time stretching out before them like the land meeting the distant horizon, and they want to do a full length CD to fill up all that extra time. 15 hours later they're still doing basics, but now that they've invested the time to lay down the songs, they just want to finish the CD. When they're in the middle of a CD project, all they can think about is having a CD to sell at their shows, and they're more than happy to buy the rest of the time at your regular rate.

Sure, most of the bands "get it," and they realize that 20 hours is about a quarter or so of the total time they'll need. They're just happy to have won the "free" studio time as a partial payment to the overall cost. This is a pretty win/win deal- the bands get studio time, you get free advertising and exposure to other bands, and the groups that win are usually pretty good. After all, they won a talent contest. And where are they going to go for their next CD? Right back to you!

Don't stop there, sponsor studio time at fundraisers and auctions. You can auction a smaller amount of time, like four hours or so. The event gets the money, you get the free advertising, and as you bath in your "community spirit" you'll look like a hero. Here's a little secret: the winners of the smaller amounts of time almost never call to set up a session. I'm knocking on wood here because I'm worried that my phone will ring tomorrow for the last ten years of my auction winners asking for their free studio time next month, but I doubt it. You can set an expiration date on it, like one or two years. Last year I raised $700 for my kid's school for four hours of time! What's the worst that can happen? They'll use the "free" time, and then they'll buy more.

Make sure you have a like button on your webpage that points back to Facebook so potential clients can "like" your Facebook page directly from the webpage. No matter how often you update your web presence, websites are very static and let's face it, kind of a pain to update. The great thing about Facebook is that when something gets posted, it shows up in everyone's newsfeed without you having to do a thing. I usually think about Facebook or ReverbNation as my daily news outlet, and the information on the somewhat clunky website I save for bigger events or for the more important news during the month. I want the look of my website to be clean and easy to read, not too cluttered.

Something I've recently discovered is giving public talks at local colleges or high schools about the music business. Engineering types aren't well known for their outgoing personalities, and maybe one reason you like being an engineer or a composer is because you often get to be by yourself. Most people would rather stare death in the face than do any form of public speaking. I'm very shy, so I'm very familiar with that feeling. The key is to talk about something you know very well. Once you start talking about something you're passionate about, you won't run out of things to say. You can talk about anything you do in the business. Maybe you teach lessons, so you can talk about how to approach your lessons and the things you've learned from students. Maybe you're a session player and want to talk about what it's like to do that kind of work. Whatever your specialty is, these talks usually last about an hour or two, and usually half of that time is question and answer. Be enthusiastic, humorous, and try and stick with stories instead of statistics. Write out what you're going to say and practice it well, just like you were practicing a piece of music to perform. But also be ready to involve the audience. Ask them questions, and encourage them to ask questions of their own. This kind of interaction makes the time fly by, and it makes the talk much more exciting. If things get slow, you can always fall back on your prepared speech.

The thing to remember is that there are real benefits to speaking in public. For one, the group that hired you to speak at their event will also publicize this speech to their mailing list, thereby getting your name out to potentially thousands more people. You can sell your merchandise at a table in the back of the room to add some revenue to your speaking fee. You also obtain "guru status" when you present at a talk or a workshop. People look up to you as the guy who knows it all, or at least the guy who knows more than they do. I usually get some work out of these events, too. Foothill College, just South of San Francisco, not only paid me to speak at a master class, but they later paid me for several guest producer sessions where I showed the students how I would run a session. I was also hired to make comments on their final projects, I've mixed several of the student CD projects outside of the school, and as a bonus I was gifted the online class time required to take the Avid Training for Pro Tools. All this from one little speaking engagement!

Usually after the talks the students are following me out to the car still asking questions. It's wonderful, and they obviously are hungry for professionals to talk to them, just like I was when I was in school.

The best news: this kind of promotion is something you just can't buy with advertising money. These presentations have been the best way to spread the word out about me and my services that I could hope for, and not only has it not cost a dime, I've been paid well for it along the way.

You can also do a weekly podcast. Hosting a show gives you some street creed. Another great thing about podcasts is that unlike music or a CD release, you can upload your podcast directly to the iTunes store without having to pay a service to do it for you. For the podcast, you can use a service like BlogTalkRadio.com, JoinMe.com, or GoToMeeting.com, where you can host a live "talk radio" style podcast where people can listen live and call in. Blogtalk radio archives and stores your show as a podcast, listeners can chat, and you can share the podcast on social networks. A basic plan is free, but as your audience gets bigger, you may want to pay a bit more for some of the premium options like the ability to edit the show later, a toll free number, more talk time, promotional elements, no banner ads, etc. If your show gets big enough, you can pursue a sponsor to help pay for the show. All you have to do to get a sponsor is convince someone that it's worth advertising on your "airwaves". Usually the sponsor can pay for basic operating expenses, and often they can pay for a lot more. The sky's the limit here. It's a very new niche market.

A weekly podcast is a lot of work, and it takes time and preparation to do it well. It helps to collaborate with different people (there's that word again) to co-host a show. That way you don't have to come up with everything. You can let the co-host for that particular week talk about what he or she does best.

A word about your studio: keep it clean. Nobody likes walking into a messy studio. Stay clean and stay organized. When you need a special cable, you need it now, and taking time to go rummaging around for it takes away from the flow of session. It's OK if the studio gets messy as the session goes throughout the day, but it needs to look good when the client first walks in. If it feels clean, the artist may be "inspired" not to make a mess with their phones, chargers, snack bags, water bottle, jackets, backpacks, and notebooks. Too much clutter can be distracting to the creative process for some people. If you're recording a band, it's just going to get messy no matter what you do with cables going everywhere, instruments laying around, pizza boxes on the producer desk, and cases stacked all over the place.

When I was designing the studio, Chips Davis told me to not make a shelf out of the window between the control room and the studio. He wanted me to put the window almost to the edge on either side. He said that if you leave a space it would just get cluttered up with crap. He was right! I just left an inch in my studio, but in that little space there's a row of pencils, some cable adaptors, two rolls of tape, some trinkets from an intern's trip to Egypt, a screwdriver and a tape measure. That crap doesn't need to be there! I'm glad the space isn't any bigger.

So how much can I expect to make as an audio engineer?

Well, that depends on a lot of factors. The real question is: can you expect to make a living doing it? Remember my first studio that I talked about earlier in the book? I charged a "dirt cheap" price when I started that studio, and that's because I was just starting out. I had crap for gear, and I had very little experience. I also had a day-job at the time and I thankfully didn't need to survive solely from the income from my little studio. Everyone will have a different situation, and their needs will change over time, but there are a few noticeable trends in the industry. Here are some interesting figures from the Bureau of Labor Statistics, and a link to the report as well.

Bureau of Labor Statistics

In the decade from 2000-2010, the median income from being a recording engineer has grown from $30,000 to $46,000, with a mean hourly wage of $22.27 per hour. $30,000 isn't much, but you also have to understand that this doesn't really give the full picture.

This information is based on the "Occupational Employment Statistics" survey, which is a form completed by businesses that have actual employees. In other words, this information doesn't account for independent people like myself, nor does it account for people that may have another job, but do some engineering on the side. Similarly, it doesn't account for people who make additional money from music doing other jobs in the industry, like composing, or licensing while they also work occasionally as an engineer. This survey only accounts for people that are hired by a company large enough to have employees. Still, it's the best source of information we have for determining the median income for our industry.

With that information, this figure seems a lot closer to the truth. That really is about what I make when you only consider only the engineering I get hired to do.

But wait. There's more! The number of jobs has also increased from 2000-2010 to the tune of 50% for audio engineers! 50% more audio jobs is a HUGE increase in the possibilities that are out there for you. The good news is that we've seen a real boom in the audio engineering field. The bad news is that this increase is expected to slow way down. The national average for the number of "civilian" jobs (jobs outside the music industry) is expected to grow by 10%-13%, but audio jobs (not A/V jobs, but "turning knobs behind a board" kind of jobs) are expected to grow only by a measly 1%.

Don't get discouraged. I specifically said that the amount of A/V jobs would continue to grow. Think about it: there's more and more video being produced every day. There are no longer just three big networks on TV, there are hundreds of television networks out there churning out segment after segment that need sound effects, voice-over, and music. Remember that everything you see on TV needs music. There are more audio books, podcasts, and internet radio than ever before, and they all need to pass through the hands of an engineer before they reach the masses. Here's a rough breakdown of what segments hire engineers:

The Motion Picture industry represents the greatest section of our workforce, hiring almost a quarter of all the audio jobs out there today. Broadcast and Cable Television comes in second, hiring 14% of all the jobs out there. There are only 14% of us who work in a recording studio setting, tying the amount of people who work in TV. Live engineers, including Sporting events, account for 12% of the jobs out there, and our little friend known as Radio only hires 4% of us.

All this is not to say that we are paid equally. The top dogs in the industry- the top ten percent of us, earn $100,000. The bottom 10% of us earn only $20,000. And there's a huge bell curve in the middle. The average wage in the United States for regular jobs was $46,000, so taking it all in, you can see that there are a lot of similarities in the pay scale between audio engineering and any other business.

The people who make the most money are in film, where an average salary is $73,000! There's still a disparity in broadcast and film, and broadcasters can expect to earn in excess of $50,000. If you want to work in live sound reinforcement or record live bands, you can hope to earn something in the $40,000 area.

You would expect that the people who hold the technological keys to actually creating the gear we use would earn more, and to no surprise, these talented guys and gals earn somewhere between $60,000 and $80,000 for their pioneering electrical and mechanical engineering work.

Another question is: where do you need to live to be able to do this kind of work? With the internet being as robust as it is these days, you can live almost anywhere to a certain degree. 45% of all the jobs out there are split between New York and California. That's a lot of jobs, and there's also a lot of competition. Some of you might do better staying in a smaller market, especially if you're just breaking into the field. You may not make quite as much as your co-workers in bigger cities, but being able to earn a comfortable living in an affordable place may be much better than living in a crowded market with an expensive mortgage. As you might expect, the other big music towns also have high concentrations of music jobs. Nashville, Austin, Seattle, and Las Vegas all employ a high number of audio people. Still, location is important, depending on the kind of work you do and the income you need to make. If you can live in L.A. and work in film, you'll be in the highest pay scale in America, earning a hefty $83,000 average per year. If you live in the South, you may expect to earn only $30,000 per year. Again- it all depends on what your living expenses are. The person making 30K may be able to keep more money than the film editor living in L.A.!

How to Charge for

Studio Time

For the studio, I typically charge by the hour. That's mostly because I learned the hard way that if you charge a flat fee for a project, the client will *never* stop wanting to work on it and make changes. Ironically, with popTuna, we typically charge a flat fee for composing music. What's the reason for that discrepancy? A lot of beginning artists don't really appreciate the effort that goes into mixing, and they often expect big budget sounds at garage band prices. When they pay by the hour, they start to understand what goes in to making a record. With popTuna, we can generally build into our fee several iterations of the finished project, and because we've allowed for these changes it's fine when a project goes a little long. We've charged for it after all. When we're talking to someone about a price for a corporate composition gig, the person calling often has to get back to a review board, and they need to know a final price. There's simply too much "red tape" to make it possible to do an hourly thing. So when a performer comes in to record and they say that they want to spend two hours on a song, I have to let them know up front what the expectations are, and what the reality is of getting a quality product with so little time and money. One of my favorite sayings is "good, fast, and cheap: pick any two."

In the pursuit of capturing great performances and sounds, the artist and I often extend a perceived two-hour session to four or even six hours or more, but I also have to be realistic and upfront as to what the client can afford, and I'm not talking just about financial terms. There's the talent issue as well. Most of us are pretty good at sizing up a person in terms of what they can do and what their limits are. Spending more time isn't necessarily going to make things better just for the sake of spending more time, and I would be doing a dis-service to my client if I'm billing them more and more time while going down a road that's leading nowhere. As long as you can com-municate where to push for more from the artist yet at the same time maintain an understanding of the scope of the project, the artist will get what they want at a price they can afford.

In a way, you can charge anything you want. Try to figure out how much you want to make in a given year, and charge accordingly. Want to make $80,000 a year? Assume there are about 2,000 work-ing hours in a year based on forty hours a week times about fifty weeks in a year. Could you simply charge $40.00 per hour and make $80,000? The catch here is that for this to work, you would have to be booked SOLID for every working hour of the year. That's just not realistic. You also have to allow for some downtime when you're ei-ther not booked or can't work, and you'll have to pad your hourly rate to accommodate this time.

Running your own business is like a full time job in itself, and then you have to do the actual engineering work for your clients on top of all that. Think about how much time you'll have to spend creating and maintaining websites, ad campaigns, schlepping gear around town to be repaired, sending out email updates, creating ads for those times when you need to do some print advertising, writing music for your library; the list goes on and on. And the to-do list *never* stops. You have to charge enough so you're financially covered when there's no client.

Some studios charge a minimum block of time, like four hours. You can purchase a bigger block of time at slightly discounted rate, such as an all day session of ten hours, where perhaps the last two hours are considered "free". If you want to book out a week, maybe the last day is free. You get the idea. You can charge a bit less for a bigger commitment of time. The good thing about doing things this way is that you don't have to scramble to fill up the time, the blocks are sold, the studio is booked, and as long as someone actually pays for the time, things run smoothly.

Interestingly enough, I don't often work this way. Let's say a new group wants to record a song, and all they want to do is rap over some pre-recorded music. They don't sing in the traditional sense, they just rap. This kind of session usually takes no more than an hour and a half, and at the most two hours. Do I sell them a four-hour block of time? I try and have them do more than one song to cover about a four-hour session, but often a new client will simply want to see what you can do for them as an engineer. I'll book them into the morning slot at 9:00, or the afternoon session at 1:00. That way, if they only use an hour or two, I can still have the other part of the day for someone else. But if they want to go for more time, there's plenty of time until my next session. Sometimes I'll cram three different quick sessions on one day so I can book the next day with someone who wants a full day. I let the artists know in advance that I only charge for the time they use, and I round the time to fifteen-minute increments. Sure, it's a bit of downtime between sessions, but with so much to deal with for the studio, I'm glad to have the time to take care of external things as they come up. This plan has also backfired on me, though. There's been a time or two where my back to back gigs have overlapped, and my next client is waiting for the current session to finish. You might think this would be a problem, but I've managed to turn this into a positive. I introduce the two performers, and they get a chance to listen to each other's tracks and make connections. What a great way for artists to get to meet!

What about getting payment in advance? Of course, you should always get payment in advance, but I almost never bother to do it. If someone is going to book the studio for a long period of time like a few days or a week, then I'll ask for half of the time as a down payment. The down payment will let you know who is serious about actually coming in and who is just gathering information. The problem is that I can almost never get an upfront payment for a project that's just coming in for a day. For these kinds of gigs, I prefer to make it a bit more casual, and then I charge my client for the time used at the end of the session. Here's the problem: a recording studio is like a restaurant with one table. If someone makes a reservation and doesn't show, the business is out of work for that time. Yes, I have a few no-shows, but as long as I thoroughly vet the person calling about the session and really understand what it is they want to do, my potential artists almost always show for the booked session. If I suspect the person calling might be one a no-show, then I'll ask for a deposit on the time. If they're serious they'll pay for the time, and if not, you've just saved yourself a no-show. Congratulations.

Now you have a few tools to help you decide about how to deal with payment: you can get a down-payment for long sessions, ask for a down-payment if you suspect they may be a no-show, and finally you can simply charge at the end of the session for shorter sessions or for returning customers who you trust will make it to their appointment.

Here's another thing about getting money up front- it takes a lot of time to convince someone to pay for time "site-unseen." More often than not they'll want to schedule a "meet and greet" session to check out the studio. This isn't really a problem, but now I have to commit some potential studio time for an unpaid meet-and-greet session, and if they actually show up, there goes another thirty minutes or so of non-recoupable income. Try to keep these "meet and greet" sessions short, but at the same time realize that you've only got this one chance to really make a connection with a potential client. If they were serious enough to haul themselves over to your studio and meet with you, chances are very good they'll choose you for their project. Depending on the scope of their venture, it may be worth it to spend a lot of extra time with them. It's just one of those things where you'll have to consider what to do when it happens.

Speaking of taking a payment for a session, how do you take a payment if they're not present to write a check or pay with cash? Here's another case where technology has come to our rescue. I have a square card reader, and I'm not afraid to use it. Here's the link to Square:

Squareup.com

Set up an account on their website, and they'll mail you a free credit card reader where you can swipe a card just like a real business directly on your mobile device! Oh wait. You are a real business! With Square, you'll be able take every major credit card, and the card reader app will transfer the money directly to your bank account. Simple. You can even take an order over the phone without swiping the card. Your client doesn't have to be present if they only want to make a deposit or pay for some something extra. Square isn't the only player out there, either. PayPal, Intuit, Chase, and several others have card readers. They all differ in terms of features, reports, and service fees, so do an online search and see what's right for you.

What if I had an employee like another engineer to run some sessions? I bet I wouldn't be able to "get away" with my passive scheduling and lackadaisical payment structure. If I had a large chunk of money going out to an engineer, I would have to be more demanding of minimum hours, more serious about up front payments, etc. I would also have to be more focused solely on the studio, and I wouldn't be able to do the other things I do like composing quite as much. For the many different kinds of jobs I do, both when a client is present and when there's not someone standing over my shoulder, this combination of both long and short session seems to work out fine for me. I'm focused during the longer sessions, and on days when I only have a short session or perhaps nobody coming into the studio on a given day, I can work on my other projects like unattended mastering sessions, jobs that come in through The MixPack, composing for film and TV, building my library of music cues, writing a book, or even simply taking care of office work. It could be argued that the demands of composing almost require a more flexible schedule, so for the solo guy who has a small studio, this type of scheduling makes a lot of sense.

PART III: How to Handle a session

Prepping for the gig

What will be expected of you when you have a session? I have several different types of gigs in the studio, and each one involves a different skillset. You don't have to be able to do everything (I sure can't), but the kind of job where you're "just" the engineer is pretty rare these days. You have to be diverse, but that's also the great thing. It keeps things interesting. I would go nuts if I had to do the same thing everyday. The famous author Robert Heinlin summed that up best for me:

"A human being should be able to change a diaper, plan an invasion, butcher a hog, pilot a ship, design a building, write a sonnet, balance accounts, build a wall, set a bone, comfort the dying, take orders, give orders, cooperate, act alone, solve equations, analyze a new problem, pitch manure, program a computer, cook a tasty meal, fight efficiently, die gallantly. Specialization is for insects."

Be upfront about what you can and can't do, and where you excel verses where you just "get by".

Still, when someone comes in to the studio to record, I feel like I have to be ready for anything. When a singer goes into the booth, I'll figure out the key of the song. I don't know if you know enough theory to know about the number system, but it's key (pun intended) to getting great sounding parts. Even if you just need to know where to optimally set Autotune for the lead vocal track, it's a huge help to know the key. What about harmonies? It helps to be able to create alternate vocal parts or at least give your singer a good place to start for ideas, plus it makes you look like a "musical genius" if you can suggest a harmony part here and there. Knowing the key of the song helps out tremendously for this. That kind of knowledge goes a long way in terms of a client returning for another day, and you'll have a real edge over the competition if you know some basic music theory and can execute it well enough.

One thing to keep in mind is that we are in a service industry. There's nothing tangible that we sell as an engineer, yet we still have to have the mindset that what we're creating in the business world is a product. Our service is a product. And like many products, there are always levels to what you buy. You can get a car that'll take you to where you want to go, or you can "supersize" and ride in style. Some people just want a demo, some need a highly produced and polished album. Be able to make a gourmet meal, but be ready to serve a cheeseburger.

One of the greatest things about providing recording services is that you are in the business of handling dreams. You're working with the one thing in the lives of your artists that's free from their jobs and their responsibilities, and handling this dream is no laughing matter. Think about it: apart from their loved ones, there's nothing more important in the lives of my clients than their music. I worked with a client whose house had burned down *the previous night*, and he still showed up for the session the following day. As his house was burning, what did he grab on the way out? Pictures? Plants? No. As soon as he knew his family was OK, he grabbed his music laptop and some hard drives with his album on it. As much as I'm a jokester in the studio and try and make people laugh, I do it to dispel the pressure placed on all of us and to invoke a creative and relaxed sense of space for the session.

Here's a break-down of the types of sessions and what will you'll need to be able to do to handle them.

The Rapper

One of the more straightforward gigs I get is the rapper who is singing over a pre-recorded instrumental, and this kind of session is the majority of my rap clientele. These sessions generally go very fast, and it's one of the few places where within an hour or two, an artist can walk out with a finished mix and master, which is very satisfying. It's easy to find free or paid instrumental rap songs. Do a search for "rap beats for sale" if they need help in finding something before they come in. It's almost always better when they write their own beats or create it at your studio. When you have access to every discrete element that makes up the song under your fingertips, you have much better control of the mix as opposed to simply having one stereo track to work with. It may take a bit more time than using a pre-mixed stereo track, but it's almost always worth it in the end.

I'm sure you're thinking that if they could make and record their own songs, why would they need a studio? Great point! Most of these guys produce the beats very well, but what they need is the $10,000 signal chain to do justice to their vocals. They can afford the free or inexpensive software to record on their laptops with the included synths and sounds, and maybe they can afford some occasional studio time. The one thing they typically can't do is afford the $3,000 mic, the $2,500 pre-amp, the $4,000 digital to analog converter, or the $4,000 sound card to get it all in the computer. Not to mention the soundproofing that goes into a studio environment. You get the picture.

Obviously, if the rapper also sings in the traditional sense, the session takes more time to nail the melodic vocal lines, and the session gets much more involved. Let's take a look at the next chapter about recording a singer songwriter, because if your rapper also sings, the line between a rap singer and a singer-songwriter gets a little blurry.

The Singer Songwriter

Another gig I often get is the singer songwriter who has original material, but needs someone to get it recorded. Generally, these gigs fall in one of three camps: someone who simply wants to have a no-frills audio document of their songs, someone who has songs and needs to either have me produce the song or put a band together to get the song recorded, and lastly, someone who has gone as far as doing some preproduction recording in their home to use in the final mix.

No matter what category they fall under, it's my job to musically "get" what it is they're doing, and turn it into a tangible sonic reality. There's that phrase again: tangible sonic reality. Sometimes I'll have to put in a bridge or fix the transition between sections so the song "flows" from one section to the next. Sometimes I'll have to play some or all the instruments and even come up with harmony parts for the vocals, all the while constantly referring to other songs from other well known artists for clarity and inspiration and growing the conversation from there. The funny thing is that even though I'm the one doing all these things in behalf of the singer, somehow the song always ends up sounding like the artist I'm working with. I would like to say that I have a chameleon-like quality as a producer and can morph into whatever I need to be, but the truth is that it's the collaboration with the artist that makes the music unique. I can't really say that I have an indelible stamp on my mixes that only sound like me. The end result sounds like what the intentions of the artist are. Ultimately, if it's a decent piece of music, I kind of feel like we're both just serving the song. The song and the artist will dictate where the energy of the piece needs to be, and as long as you "serve the song" or let the song be the guide, I feel like things will typically sound unique. As a producer, you'll have to discover on your own what's going to work for you, and a lot of it depends on what kind of work you end up doing. For example, a DJ/producer may need to have a sonic imprint from project to project, but a producer like myself may need to be more variable in their sound.

A "documentary" session is in a way similar to the rapper sessions. If the artist simply wants a recording of just their instrument and the vocals, then we can record the instrument and the vocal at the same time. Once we find the sound for the guitar or piano and carefully set up the mics, these sessions generally go very fast. You can often do an entire album in a day if it's truly a very stripped down recording. Another option here is that you can initially record just the instrument, such as guitar or piano, and then later we'll do the vocal as an overdub. Some artists can do one without the other, but not everyone can do them separately. Look at it this way: these artists have been playing both parts so often that the "muscle memory" is difficult to disconnect unless they practice it this way. If you do the vocal as an overdub, you then open yourself to being able to use things like AutoTune for the vocals. If there's too much acoustic guitar bleed in the vocal mic, or too much vocal bleed in the guitar mics, AutoTune tends to get "flanged" sounding with the non-tuned guitar tracks.

Let's talk about cases where a client comes in and they don't have a band, and maybe doesn't even have chords worked out for the track, and as a stretch might not even play an instrument. Why would anyone come into a studio if they don't play an instrument? It happens a lot! These kinds of singer-songwriter sessions start out with a bang. I grab my easily accessible acoustic guitar that I hang on the wall, and within a few minutes we have the song mapped-out with a rough chord structure. Whatever new sections need to be composed are created and transitions are fixed.

Even if you're working with an accomplished songwriter/player, it's still a good idea to get a rough version of the song mapped out in your DAW (Digital Audio Workstation) of choice. We'll typically figure out the tempo, create a click track or a drum part, and record a rough version of song- even if it's just my talk-back mic channel with the artist in the control room. Sometimes we'll go for "the" acoustic guitar or piano take on this inceptive rough pass. For me, being able to see the song on screen helps to visualize the track, especially since we can label the sections. If you're going to record the instrumental take, try and visualize how that instrument needs to function in the song. If it's a complicated mix, will the acoustic be panned to one speaker to make room for other instruments? If so, there goes trying to depend solely on a figure eight technique for the guitar sound. If you have a good picture of the song before you record anything, you can make some decisions like how bright or boomy the guitar sound needs to be in terms of mic placement. Sure- you can usually re-record the guitars if needed, but it's great when you don't *have* to.

Once you have the song mapped out, then the routine of recording begins. Mostly for timing and feel, I'll start with a basic drum part if I didn't already create it for a fancy click track. I wish I could say that I play drums well enough to record (OK, I wish I played drums at all) because there's just no substitute for real drums played by a good drummer. More on that in a minute. I usually work with Superior Drummer, but use whatever program you feel comfortable with. Then we start laying down each part- bass, acoustic, overdubs, electric guitars, percussion, keys, whatever the song needs.

I also do a something that's a bit out of the norm, I like to somewhat mix as we go. You never know what the song needs until you hear it played back, and the playback has to sound mixed to give an accurate picture of the song. I'm not talking about a fully mix and mastered production here, I'm just talking about having the sounds more or less finalized either as you record them, or finding the sound before you record the next thing. As a singer, there's nothing worse than trying to emote over a flat sounding, uninspiring track. In a perfect world, everything you record will more or less sound great *as it's recorded*, and no plug-ins or effects (except maybe reverb or some other time domain effect) will be needed. I had to learn this approach with my original crappy set-up, but it taught me an awful lot about capturing the sounds correctly before you hit "record." Getting the right sounds can also be translated as getting cool sounds, and cool sounds inspire other things to happen. Plus, if things already sound good before you mix, think about how much faster the mix will go!

Latency is always an issue no matter what DAW you're working in, and if you have the signal chain going through a lot of plug-ins, then you run the risk of having timing errors in the performances.

Hopefully by the time you're ready to record the vocals, you have a slammin' track that's going to provide the motivation for the singer. I'm always saying that there's nothing more important than the vocals, and if they're singing to something that's going to move them, your great sounding mix overcomes a big hurdle before it becomes a problem.

Once the lyrics are recorded, it's time for mixing and then mastering, and the client is out the door. Here's where the financial end of things gets interesting. If the artist had to pay for a studio and an engineer, that's one price, more or less, right? Some places will charge separately for an engineer. If the artist had to pay for each instrumentalist, that could get very expensive. Sure, the artist could hire a drummer, a bass player, and a guitarist, which I advise to do by the way, but it's getting less and less common that a person without a band or some other source of financial relief can afford to do this kind of thing. My experience has been that it's much better when a professional drummer or bass player comes in and all they do is play drums or bass. Chances are these instrumentalists are going to come up with a much better and more interesting part than I'm ever going to get on my own. And usually the project just won't sound as "cool" or organic unless the parts are from real instruments. But it costs a lot of money to get a room full of pros together. Just by charging a small "producer fee" above the regular cost of the studio, I can get the job done affordably for the client, a job that would in a lot of cases never have been possible if you had to hire out a group of other musicians. I only offer this kind of thing after I've exhausted the possibility of hiring "real" musicians. Nothing beats real people playing together, and I love it when I can get work for my friends.

These singer-songwriter gigs are some of my favorites. Not only do they pay a little more, but I get to use all my chops to get the music recorded. I'm super involved with the production. It's a real team effort and time just flies by.

Recording a Band

Recording bands keeps me very busy as an engineer. The demands that are placed on the gear in this case separate what a project studio can do verses what a bigger facility can do. 16 tracks at once is the bare minimum of tracks you you'll need to record a live band. I typically use 12 or more tracks just for the drums, and that's even considered low! You have to have a fairly large mic locker, an ample supply of DI boxes, a way to have multiple simultaneous mixes for headphones because everyone will want more "me", a way for everyone to see each other while they're performing, plenty of sturdy mic stands, and miles and miles of cables. Take this with a grain of salt: I used to only be able to record two tracks at once, and look what the Beetles did with four tracks.

When the band arrives, there seems to be an expectation that everything has to happen at once. You can always tell when people haven't recorded very often. They don't know about how much time it takes to get things up and running. A lot of people want to start recording as soon as they arrive without realizing that they first have to get everyone set up and dialed in. To make things flow a bit smoother, I always have my microphones, headphones and direct boxes set up and line checked *before* the band arrives. The last thing I have the time or patience for is crawling over instrument cases and running cables everywhere in a crowded room. Even with careful set-up, there will always be enough surprises to keep you busy no matter how much planning you've done in advance.

A note about click tracks: If the band can play with a click, and if the song is supposed to stay at a constant tempo, then by all means, use a click track! Not every band can play to a click. Playing to a click is yet another musical skill, and mastering the technique can take years of practice. It can seriously suck the life out of some projects if the band isn't accustomed to it, and some songs simply have to change tempo at some point.

It takes a while to set up and get good sounds, get the headphone mixes set up, and to get everybody comfortable. For me, things calm down when the recording starts, and I can just concentrate on the music. There are still things to keep me busy, like checking for any technical problems that arise, taking notes about takes, hopefully enjoying the music (that's what it's all about, right?), but in general, once the band is recording and things are flowing, there's not much to do beyond listening, paying attention, and making notes about what may need to get fixed. Sure, I'll also smile, nod enthusiastically, mosh, whatever I can do to encourage the band and promote a sense of fun and encouragement to the session.

Overdubs get a little more hands-on, and I can be more involved in terms of what I think was a good take, as long as they want my opinion. Overdubs are great. I finally get to be one-on-one with the musician and see what they're like musically apart from the band. It's sort of the "what can you do when no-one's looking" kind of thing. The other nice thing about recording an overdub is that you really get to concentrate on the part that's being added. There's no other instrument or musician that you have to pay attention to. You can finally focus on the task at hand and not be too distracted by anything else happening.

Things get really interesting for me during mixing. I'm quite fast with Pro Tools and all their short cuts, and when clients see me work they immediately feel like they're in good hands. Get fast on your DAW and learn the shortcuts! Hopefully you don't have to mix on the same day you do the basics. My ears need a break, and after a full day of basics I'm pretty spent. Usually, there're just a few members of the band present when you mix, which is hopefully a bit more calm in contrast to the basics session. If the whole band is there, suddenly I'm in a room full of incredibly loud people trying to mix music, which is like trying to read braille on a stucco wall. How do you make a room full of people be quiet? Instead of asking them to be quiet, ask them what they think of <u>blank</u> and list any tiny part of the sound, say the snap of the kick, or the high end of the vocal. While they're listening, you can get some real work done.

If I'm hired on as the producer- and it's understood exactly WHAT I'm to be doing as a producer from the start, I can have a bit more input for the album. Even before the band walks in for the basics, hopefully I've received a rough recording of a rehearsal, and from there I can create a plan about how to record the song. But suddenly the buck stops here. If the kick and bass guitar parts aren't happening, it's my fault now, and I have to fix it if the band doesn't, or at least I have to suggest that there may be an issue. I like to stay out of the way and let the band be the band, but if there's something happening that I feel is detrimental, then it's my job to say something, and the earlier I mention it the better.

Sometimes I won't know what's happening with the kick and bass parts until I hear a quality version of it in the studio. In fact, band members often remark that they haven't heard the part the other guy's doing before because they haven't yet heard it clearly. If we need to change something, we have to figure out what to do "on the spot" and fix it in the basics, but time is not on your side. The clock is ticking- whether I'm charging by the hour or by the project. It's a little dicey when there's something I know that needs to be fixed, but the band isn't into fixing it for whatever reason. I'm not going to force a decision onto a band, but as a producer, I would be "in the wrong" if I didn't at least bring it up. It would be different if I had *hired* a band, and they were obligated to do it, but I have to respect the overall vision of the band. Who knows, their idea just might work out after all!

The Home Musician/Engineer

Often a client will bring in tracks they've recorded at home and they just need a mix and master. Usually (and I mean almost down to the person), they also want to learn about *how* to mix better, and they want to sit in on the session with me. I might be the only guy in history who actually likes to have people sitting over my shoulder as I mix. I like having the immediate feedback from the client, and since they're the writer/composer, no one will know better what they want to have happen in the mix. As long as they're not too pressed for cash, and can sort of "go the extra mile," then we can keep pushing for better and better results. For example, you can always bring more low end out of the kick, and then once you've gone too far, you can always bring out more of the *right* kind of low end. The cool thing is that they get to see how intricate a big mix can be, and how they need to invest some serious cash in gear if they want to be able to do it themselves, which ultimately is another argument for them to bring their tracks to a professional studio to mix in the first place. I'll show them everything I'm doing until they're sick of hearing about it, and I'll answer questions as they come up. Plus, I get to learn a lot in the process, too. It's a bit of a collaborative effort when you work along side someone, and even if you're simply improving their mix, it's good to see how someone else approaches the exact same problem. These sessions are typically win-win. The client walks away feeling like they got a whole lot more than just a mix, and they usually leave with a little more respect for what I do, too.

Do I ever feel like I'm educating away my clients? Well, if someone is going to mix on their own, there's nothing I can do to stop them. Come hell or high water, they're going to do it at home, just like I did. I also think that there aren't too many artists who can balance the technical side and the creative side to the degree to which they no longer seek outside help, at least at some point along the way. There are so many things you have to do as an artist. Who has the time to learn how to record, then mix, and then master on top of writing, performing, and managing the rest of their career? It's true, there are a lot of people who have day jobs and are musicians on the side, but if you have a 9-5 job every day, it gets tough to find the time to learn a skill like songwriting or engineering on top of being an artist. Get help if you can, no matter what side of the glass you're working on. You would be amazed at how much you can learn from another person even if you only work with them on one song.

Voice Overs

Voice-Over projects are interesting because the talent is usually top-notch and professional, and I can generally charge my corporate rate. One would think that a VO session would be one of the easiest gigs in history, especially compared to having a band in the studio where everyone wants everything right from the start, but oddly enough I find these sessions quite intense.

There's simply no down time. The time between takes is quite short, the talent quickly gets tired if it's a lot of VO work, and the job of keeping the energy up the entire time falls completely on you. There's no vivacious band this time around creating a party atmosphere. There's a huge volume of takes, often many alternate takes for the same part, and there's a bunch of tiny but important details to take care of. Even though I'm rarely the producer on these gigs, there's a lot of pressure to get things happening quickly. Sometimes there are several people scheduled in quick succession, and things have to move along fast.

The trick to voice over work is "asset management." Sometimes there are hundreds if not thousands of audio clips that have to be delivered, especially for game audio. Keeping up with these takes and naming them is a daunting task. Sometimes the game company has a specific naming structure for the files, but if you use your own format, you have to be specific and consistent. Name the files between takes if you can. What do I mean by that? Say we're doing a film project for an animated movie, and the character we're recording is used throughout the film. Hopefully the film is labeled well, such as by scene number, or better yet *line* number. With Pro Tools, how-ever you label your track will be reflected in the file name, so for example for scene 37, line 15, you can label your track "sce-ne_37_line15." Whenever you loop record the audio to match the animation, all the takes will be labeled correctly. The next scene will obviously have a different set of numbers, so they can be easily dis-tinguished from scene to scene. When you literally have 1000 takes to rename because you forgot to label the track for each take, you learn this lesson pretty fast. I usually move the "keeper" takes to an-other track to export later, and I give the client both a folder of all the carefully chosen takes and a copy of the entire "Audio Files" folder if they later decide they want to use a different performance.

I know how redundant this sounds, but it also helps to have the producer present at the session. I find that I'm so busy taking care of the engineering and file labeling management that I rarely have the time or mental capacity to know whether or not it was a good take or if (and this is important) the correct words were spoken. Did the tal-ent add an extra "the" or leave out an "s" that needs to be there? Having an extra person or two around to catch these tiny details is a great idea in these circumstances, especially when I'm so distracted.

Not all VO gigs are the same, and they all require different la-bels and delivery requirements. Ultimately you have to find the best workflow for you, but it's always best to be very clear up front about what it is that needs to be delivered.

Film Mixing

I work with a handful of documentary filmmakers. These sessions are similar to the guy who records at home, and just needs me to mix something. Except in this case, I have to fix their bad dialog edits, clean up the background noise, and add room tone when a scene changes. I usually have to brighten poorly recorded sections of audio, fix the places where they looped the music *not* on beat, get a general mix on things, you name it. A lot of times the director/editor didn't even know they had an audio problem on the rough mix until they listened back on a nice speaker system. They often say something like "It sounds great on my computer, why does it sound bad here? Does your gear suck?" I have to remind them that they are used to listening back on their tiny one inch laptop speakers with no low end, and that a lot of people have really nice TV's with audio going through a high end playback system. So let's fix it! It's got to sound good on just about any system. I think for a film, the dialogue is king, just like in a song where the vocals are the most important thing. I like to get the dialogue working before anything else, so I'll make sure the room tone doesn't jump in or out too much, and the transitions from scene to scene are smooth. I'm a pretty big music fan. I don't watch a ton of TV (well, not enough in terms of R&D for the kind of work I do). But I keep noticing the same thing over and over: one thing that drives me crazy is when the music is so loud that you can't hear the dialog. It doesn't take much music for that to happen, but it seems like there could be a better balance out there. I try and make sure the music in my film mixes support the voice on the film. There's an an-

126

imated TV series called "Family Guy" that takes this to an extreme. They never have music over a voice, or if they do, it's there for a very good reason. As a result, their sound is clean, clear, and understandable.

One thing that has come a long way in terms of all the different DAW's working together is OMF (Open Media Format) import and export. For years there was no way for a video editor to export their audio files in way that could later be edited on another program. Sure, the editor could always (and still can) export a single file mix of each row of audio tracks in their video project, but being able to have "handles" to reveal or extend and audio track *beyond their edit* is a dream come true. Editors have to cut video- it's their job, after all. Unfortunately, the audio that goes with the scene they're cutting isn't always at the ideal place for audio. Sometimes there's an audible click or pop, sometimes the audio ends abruptly or oddly, and sometimes the room tone goes quiet and suddenly reappears. With an OMF file, I can extend their audio cuts and make my own decisions about where the audio should transition from one cut to another. OMF has a long way to go in terms of true interoperability between DAWs, but I'm grateful for even its most basic ability of being able to transfer audio tracks back and forth between programs. Perhaps we'll see the day when Logic can read Pro Tools automation, or Digital Performer will be able to understand the plug-in settings of Final Cut as translated through OMF. OMF works for several different DAWs, too: Digital Performer, Pro Tools, Logic, and Final Cut are just a few of the programs that can transfer files this way.

Mastering

I like doing mastering work, and it's great to take a completed project that a band is happy with and making it sound even better. My rule of thumb is that you should *definitely* not master where you mix, and I try to dissuade my clients from having me master their projects if we've mixed at my place. When you master where you mix, especially if it's at your own studio, you'll always print the same sonic "signature" you make when you mix, for better or (usually) worse. You'll also be battling the same sonic tuning issues in your mixing room. Even the best million dollar mastering facilities have room tuning issues, and I'm just guessing that your control room is no better. So when the final board mix has too much low end in the car because your near field monitors can't reproduce anything below 50Hz, just imagine what happens when you master in the same room with the same gear, potentially multiplying the frequencies that are already too present, and diminishing the ones that need to be more present. When you send your mastering work out to another location, you get another set of ears, another set of speakers in a different room, and another opinion about how things should sound.

If you can swing it, go somewhere that *only* does mastering. They'll probably do a better job than what a multi-use facility like mine can do. Since they don't have to buy a whole rack of pre-amps, a nice big multichannel mixer, or invest in a huge mic locker, they can focus their financial resources on buying the $4000.00 EQ, stereo tube compressor, and mastering grade speakers. Plus, most mastering engineers, the ones that more or less only do mastering, are "aurally tuned" for mastering, as opposed to a producer who has to look at a different "whole picture," so these guys and gals are going to catch things that most mere mortals might miss. This is one of those rare cases where perhaps specializing in a niche might be a better way to go as an engineer. There are three mastering guys I totally trust in the Bay Area: Ken Lee in Oakland, Gary Hobish in Berkeley, and Michael Romanowski in San Francisco. I wouldn't think of sending my clients to anyone else. These guys (and their teams) just master, they've been doing it forever, and they are *very* good at it.

Here's the funny thing: most of my clients, the ones who are kind of new to recording, always want me to master their projects. Despite everything I just said, I'll often take the gig. I know I just said that it was a bad thing to do. True, and like I said, I really try and talk my artists out of having me do it. I have business cards on hand for my suggested mastering engineers, I have glossy magazine covers with articles and pictures about these guys that I present to my clients, I tell them what you just read a minute ago. I do everything I can do to make them go somewhere else. Remember when I was saying that sometimes they just want a cheeseburger? Maybe they just want to be finished, or maybe they just want to work with someone they trust. Whatever the reason is, unless they have the experience to know better, they still often want to do it quickly and conveniently under one roof.

How does it turn out when you master where you mix? Despite my warnings about doom and gloom, and as long as you more or less know what you're doing, the mastering will still turn out fine.

You already know how to correct for the issues in your mixing space. Hopefully you had most of them dealt with when you had your room tuned. You can listen to other commercially mastered songs in your space to know what it needs to sound like. Just import other commercial CDs into your DAW and A/B their mixes against your mixes. That process should reveal quite a lot about your sound. Listen in the car, in your living room, on your laptop, everywhere you can go to make sure your mastering mixes will translate into the "real world." Still, try to push your clients into going somewhere else. My CD projects just sound better to my ear when they are mastered at another location.

If you do the mastering yourself, just remember that the duplication house isn't going to listen to your CD to make sure everything is right. You are the last person that will error-check the CD. Unless you have a "hidden song" on the CD, it's up to you to ensure that the number of songs on the disc equals the number of intended tracks for the project. I've made this mistake before. You also have to make sure the song titles are entered correctly, the ISRC codes are in place and lots of other tiny details you have to check and double check before the CD leaves for the duplicator.

Should you attend the mastering session if you master elsewhere? I like to go whenever I can. I always learn a lot, and I get to say hello to some of my mastering friends. I look at it like an educational field trip. On the other hand, it's nice to be "on call" back at the studio in case the band quickly needs a new vocal up mix, the kick turned up, less high hat or whatever. These kinds of changes are typically very easy and fast to make, and I can upload the new mix in a matter of minutes with Hightail, Dropbox, FTP, or any other such service. A lot of mastering engineers don't like the engineer being present anyway. Who can blame them? I don't like a lot of people talking and making noise in my studio when I'm doing some very serious critical listening either!

Composing

When the studio isn't booked, there's usually some composing work to fill in the time. Even if there's no actual gig happening, you always need to build up your library. Poptuna is great. We just write music and sometimes we create sound design. There's nothing like making a scene come alive through music and sound design. Even if you're just working with talking heads on a screen, the "what" they are talking about will need a vibe or a feeling, and putting life into these kinds of visuals is intensely satisfying.

You would think that for something as important as the audio, we would have a huge say in pre-production, but typically we only get a very quick description of what the client is looking for in any given video project. In a perfect world, we get pulled into the film very early on, and we can create music before any video is captured. Often by the time the client gets us involved, the "creatives" at the ad agency (or wherever the project has come from) have already figured out what mood they want, and maybe they've put in a temporary piece of music in the commercial. Temp music is the bane of our existence. No matter how horrid or great the temp music is, once the client has seen the spot with the temp music, the temp music is what the client will forever expect to hear. So, if the client wants to hear the temp track music, then why isn't the temp track used for the final version? There are a few very good reasons for this: One is that if the temp track is composed by a well known artist, the agency may be afraid that it would be too expensive to license the song. Unless they're using a mega-star level artist for the temp track music, this is usually an utter fallacy. Almost any artist would be willing to license a song for a commercial or film project for a reasonable budget, and I'm betting that almost any composer would grant permission for a lot less money than what you're being paid to compose the music! Another good reason that most companies don't go with the temp track is that they have no idea about how to license a song, and they are afraid of the potential legal ramifications of going about it the wrong way. They've never heard about a compulsory license, which states that a "company seeking to use a patent can do so without seeking the patent holder's consent, and pays the patent holder a set fee for the license." I've even gone as far as to show some of my clients this link, but they still won't want to touch anything that has anything to do with the word "legal" in it. I completely understand.

Here's the link to "Compulsory License".

Compulsory License

Going back to the video project at hand, and being the fine, upstanding member of the musical community that I am (ahem,

ahem), I feel like my initial knee-jerk impulse to a visual is the best thing I'm going to come up with. Hey, I'll never get another chance to respond to it for the first time. If they've started an initial pass and have fallen in love with the temp music that's already embedded, chances are they'll "shot down" our first pass knee-jerk response and ask for something much closer, maybe even identical to the temp track. Seriously! No matter how good our initial music pass is, the client will still expect to hear the temp track. That's no fault of their own, really. The editor can't present anything to the client without music, and remember, everything you see on TV needs music! If the editor is good at what he or she does, chances are the music direction will at the very least be a *decent* choice, and the client is not going to get another chance to see and hear it for the first time, either. To make a long story short, we'll sometimes have to copy the temp track for our second iteration. If we've done our job really well in terms of engineering, they'll say it's too close to the temp track. Now we're in a very good position to make some real positive changes. Over the next few musical passes we can slowly turn the boat around and head toward the direction we were heading in the first place.

Although in all fairness, I have to say that most of the time we really do get a much better piece by the time we go through these multiple revisions. No really, I'm not bitter! Without getting too philosophic, the music you write is your legacy. You want it to be the best it can be, it will outlive all of us, after all. Sure, all this back and fourth can be a little bit frustrating, but by the time we've all gone through the process, everyone involved feels totally solid about the final result.

Here's a funny thing about music and sound. Remember that saying about video without audio being technical difficulties? Too many film projects deal solely on the visual aspect, and this is especially true if there are special effects shots. I did a commercial for an unnamed company where every shot was intense CG, and music was the *last* thing they wanted to think about. Finally, as the deadline was rapidly approaching, they were at last willing to begin to pay attention to the music. I know. It seems counterintuitive to wait until the last possible second for something as important as sound, but get used to it. Despite how integral audio is to any film project, we audio guys are simply considered "second class citizens." Oh well, at least the gigs pay pretty well.

We've also had some very difficult gigs, too. We've had our fair share of people wanting to change something just so they can feel like they were there for a reason. Maybe they feel like they need to make a change so they can justify their jobs, maybe they just need to push someone around. Whatever the issue, we've had a few sessions where the piece was nailed. Everyone knew it, and at the last minute a producer walks in and says something like "this needs to be in ¾" or "We need a Sousaphone for the lead line" or "We need Johnny Cash to sing this part" (even though he passed away years ago). Are these guys crazy? Absolutely, unless the ¾ comment is because the documentary is about Waltzes, or the sousaphone line is because the piece is about John Philip Sousa. Perhaps there's a reason why the producers said what they said. Find out what that was all about. If it truly is a crazy demand, hopefully it's something that can be done when they leave. When you later turn in the same piece of music that you presented earlier, say that you loved their ideas, and now that their ideas have been implemented in the piece, it's ready to go. Once you've justified their job security to another person in the company, they'll come back to you for the next gig!

Part IV: Get Busy

The Fate of Recording Studios.

One topic that I want to talk about is the fate of the recording studio. Except in a few circumstances, recording studios are dying away. The concept of what a recording studio should be is dramatically changing. Sure, some of you reading this book might find work in a large format studio somewhere. Someone may have a recurring gig where their studio is often booked and needs to hire some extra help, or maybe you can get a job at or own a large enough studio that records live bands or orchestral gigs. Orchestras will always need to be recorded, and there will always be a *need* for large-scale studios to some degree. Unless you're super wealthy and own a massive studio space, I think that the real value of your services will not be as a recording studio owner, but as a producer, engineer, or a composer. My studio space is *tiny*, so I don't spend too much time worrying about marketing "the studio." Instead, I try to market myself. The artist is looking for someone to take their vision and make it happen, and I market myself as being the competent engineer and producer they are looking for. The space I work in is adequate enough, but the space alone isn't going to fill the calendar. It's the talents that I bring to the table that's going to get the gig.

The music biz is changing so much right now. To survive you must be able to roll with the changes. I remember talking to an engineer back in the mid 90's who worked with Monica and was a partner at Annex Studios. He was talking about how Pro Tools had "ruined" recording, and the Annex was in trouble financially. He was complaining that there were all these guys with ADATs and Pro Tools rigs thinking they can record bands. He was right. We could record bands, and eventually that kind of thinking created a whole revolution in recording technology.

OK. Hindsight is 20/20. They had a too much of an overhead to continue doing business they way they had been for decades, and they needed to change their marketing approach. True, they couldn't compete price-wise with smaller studios with Pro Tools rigs, but they failed to realize that they didn't have to. It's not always about money. You *know* this to be true. Think about selling CDs today verses being able to get it for free from the internet. How do you compete with free? Think about that every time you pass a vending machine that sells water for two dollars per bottle. The studio in Menlo Park eventually managed to change what it was doing. It wound up getting a gig where they did sound design for a major toy company, and became once again very successful. Sure, it still records bands, too.

On a positive note

I don't know if you remember when the desktop publishing revolution happened. With Photoshop, suddenly everyone could produce wonderful looking printed material right in the convenience of their own home! Wow! The only problem here was that for the majority of people, it *looked* like it was done in their house. It takes a real pro to get professional results, and the same is true in the audio world. Most bands out there have at least one member that owns a recording rig of some sort. Why would these bands need a studio? Usually, they find out pretty quick why they need a professional mix, or why their drums sound like cardboard, and especially why their mixes sound so quiet in their car. They need at least a small to mid-sized studio that has someone who knows what he or she is doing with a large number of discrete recording channels. Here's the funny thing. I love for my clients to record at home. I encourage them to do it. I think I get more biz from it. My clients are better educated about audio so they have more realistic expectations. They record more and then they need me more often. Plus, they have a little more respect for what I do, and their material is often better because they're doing it more and more. When we actually use the tracks they recorded at home, they feel like everyone is part of the team.

Anyway, things are changing. I briefly said the concept of a recording studio was dying, but here's where things get exciting. There are a gazillion different ways to be able to do some sort of studio work, and there are a lot of "outside the box" type of gigs that also pay very well. This isn't anything new. Remember my friend Charlie the cinematographer who worked at GE and ended up creating several in-house videos? He managed to switch his career without ever leaving his job! It seems like every major company has a need to produce in-house videos for training, fundraising, or community outreach. These companies, both large and small, need music, voice-over, editing, etc. They need YOU. Recording set-ups are so darn affordable these days, and if you're already working at a mid to large company, it's easy (well, easy-ish) to request the money to get some sort of recording set-up, and they need people like yourself to make it all happen. Even Poptuna works with a bunch of corporate places like Johns Hopkins University and the Wall Street Journal doing some "outside the box" kind of composing gigs. They hire us to compose music for their fundraising and event videos, trade shows, and training videos. In short, there's a ton of work that's outside of the "normal" places that need your services.

A few years ago I played guitar on a track for Guitar Hero ("God of War" the metal version), and I had to go to SONY in Foster City to do the recording. It's actually SCEA, which stands for SONY Computer Entertainment America. I'm thinking about all the money that video Games make, and here I'm on my way to SONY expecting this huge recording facility. Their main room wasn't much bigger than my control room. OK, the drum room was fairly large, but the control room was just a room with a rack of mic pres and a D-command from Avid. It looked and sounded nice, though. Then I remembered: if it sounds good, it is good, and this is all you ever need. In the main room SECA had a producer, one main engineer, and a few interns. Wouldn't you like to have the main engineer's job! The cool thing is they also have eleven little "pod" studios, composing rooms where the "musical creators/editors" (for lack of a better word) can play the game and create or augment the music whenever they need it. They have a ton of hard drives all networked together so each pod has access to all the source music that's been created, all networked together with Pro Tools. These "pods" are really just networked edit bays, each equipped with a Pro Tools HD rig, a small Yamaha DM1000 digital mixer, 5.1 surround sound, and some M-Audio keyboard controllers. It's a very simple and cost effective way to produce a large volume of music.

Here's another interesting thing: Just like any major film, SECA also has a need for orchestral recording dates, so they book a few days at Skywalker Ranch or Abbey Road to record. Once the orchestra is recorded, they then take all the full orchestral short and long cues, sections, etc, and start inserting these cues into the game. Then it's up to the composers in the pods to make it all come together for a great gaming experience. The point about all this is that it's the breakdown into smaller and smaller studios that has become the norm. Even SONY hires out for the big orchestral dates. It doesn't need to own a large recording facility. Even though it may seem disappointing that working in a big studio is less and less the norm, who cares! There's a lot more work out there now. Instead of one guy getting the job at SONY, there are now about 14 or 16 guys who have the audio jobs at SONY, and that's just in Foster City. SONY also has another office in Santa Monica. And they hire out for other special things, too.

You don't have to wait for Taxi to forward your stuff to the music libraries. You can contact them yourself and send them your material. Open up your local version of the Reel Directory and get yourself in front of the people making films, and let them know that you can make their scene come alive. Get a job as the audio guy in an advertising agency. Better yet, create that job. Start teaching recording at a music store. Get your name out there and get your studio booked!